"For most of us, the enormous monolith of the suffering of Africa is impossible to imagine, much less enter into. This book represents a significant door. It is a precious gift from two women, both uniquely qualified to speak for the suffering children of Uganda, one an eloquent survivor and the other a fearless advocate. It is no coincidence that their names are Grace and Faith."

—**Michael Card**, Bible teacher and musician

"*Girl Soldier* is not fiction, yet that fact becomes harder to believe with every page we turn. How did we not know about this sooner? Why are we not doing more? This book is more than just a call to action. It is a challenge to our moral compass. Grace and Faith have made it very clear that for more than twenty years we have turned our backs on an entire generation of children. What is equally clear is that all hope is not lost. Grace's story of resiliency and peace is the light that can guide us all."

—**Adrian Bradbury**, founder and director, GuluWalk

"A much-needed reminder of the suffering and faith of the people of northern Uganda. Both have gone largely unnoticed for too long."

—**The Rt. Rev. Robert W. Duncan**, bishop, Episcopal Diocese of Pittsburgh; moderator, Anglican Communion Network

"After reading this book, I will never be the same. The story of Grace Akallo and the brutality against children in Uganda is hard for me as an American, living comfortably, to imagine—but it is real and continuing. The world has ignored these innocent children for decades, as the turmoil in Uganda has escalated into one of the world's biggest humanitarian crises. Yet this is a story of hope and a simple challenge to us all: *Help!* Our prayers and our finances can be life-changing for thousands in Uganda, and pressure on our government to intervene can alter the course of that nation forever. Thank you, Grace and Faith, for sharing your stories and for calling us to love and to act on behalf of those who cannot help themselves."

—**Robbie Seay**, Sparrow Records recording artist and songwriter

"Faith McDonnell has given a precious gift in the story of Grace Akallo. Their book serves as a poignant reminder that the darkness of the soul and the cruel behaviors it leads to are more devastating than we could imagine. Apart from the ignorance and indifference of the world to the plight of children caught in violence, there is still One who understands and redeems. Hope can grow and flourish from even the most broken of seeds. This is an incredible account that demands a hearing and invites a response."

—**Steven W. Haas**, vice president, World Vision International

"*Girl Soldier* is a moving account of a people's suffering and a girl's extraordinary faith. In a unique format, the book moves back and forth between the narrative arc of Grace Akallo's life and the historical roots of the northern Uganda tragedy. But this is not just a story of victimization; rather, it illuminates the resiliency of the human spirit. Providentially, the namesakes of the two authors, Faith McDonnell and Grace Akallo, underscore the theme of this book—that in spite of unimaginable terror, faith and grace abound."

—**Allen Hertzke**, professor of political science and director of religious studies, University of Oklahoma; author, *Freeing God's Children: The Unlikely Alliance for Global Human Rights*

girl soldier

A Story of Hope for Northern Uganda's Children

FAITH J. H. MCDONNELL
AND GRACE AKALLO

Chosen
Grand Rapids, Michigan

© 2007 by Faith J. H. McDonnell and Grace Akallo

Published by Chosen Books
A division of Baker Publishing Group
P.O. Box 6287, Grand Rapids, MI 49516-6287
www.chosenbooks.com

Printed in the United States of America

Library of Congress Cataloging-in-Publication Data
McDonnell, Faith J. H.
    Girl soldier : a story of hope for northern Uganda's children / Faith J. H. Mc-
Donnell and Grace Akallo.
        p.   cm.
    Includes bibliographical references and index.
    ISBN 10: 0-8007-9421-4 (pbk.)
    ISBN 978-0-8007-9421-7 (pbk.)
    1. Uganda—Church history. 2. Girls—Crimes against—Uganda. 3. Abduc-
tion—Uganda. 4. Uganda—Politics and government. 5. Akallo, Grace.
    I. Akallo, Grace. II. Title.
BR1443.U33M33 2007
276.761'0829—dc22   2007000168

Unless otherwise indicated, Scripture is taken from the HOLY BIBLE, NEW INTER-
NATIONAL VERSION®. NIV®. Copyright © 1973, 1978, 1984 by International Bible
Society. Used by permission of Zondervan. All rights reserved.

Scripture marked NKJV is taken from the New King James Version. Copyright © 1982
by Thomas Nelson, Inc. Used by permission. All rights reserved.

Photos on pp. 33, 123, 132, 135, 144, 147, 155 by Sarita Hartz. Hartz, of Arlington,
Virginia, has begun a new initiative for the victims of northern Uganda's war and displacement called Zion Project. Zion Project is a grassroots, faith-based project with a
mission of grace: To revolutionize war-affected communities whose needs are unmet by
humanitarian aid through intimate healing, creative empowerment, and holistic transformation in the lives of the most vulnerable—girl child
soldiers, child mothers, and refugees in Africa. The mission
hopes to provide an after-care shelter for child mothers (a
trauma center that will provide deep heart transformation
through counseling) and agricultural development within
a resettled IDP [internally displaced persons] camp.

I dedicate this book to my wonderful husband, Francis, and my precious daughter, Fiona, who put up with many months of my being even busier than usual. They make my world more beautiful and joyful than I could ever imagine. I realize every day how grateful I am to God for them.

—Faith

First I dedicate this book to God, who gave me the gift of life, protected me and gave me His love.

I dedicate this book to the Aboke girls who were abducted from St. Mary's College. All these innocent children suffered under the brutality of Kony and his LRA, yet with faith they believe in God's love and care. I pray that those whose lives were cut short will find peace in the hands of God.

I dedicate this book to Sister Rachele, who with great love risked her own life to rescue the Aboke girls. She managed to rescue 109 out of 139, and she continued to ask for help for the remaining 30 girls.

I also dedicate this book to Sister Alba, who was the headmistress at the time I was abducted. She never stopped praying for the Aboke girls and all the children abducted by the rebels. When she went to Italy, she said, "Children, I am going to the mountain to pray for you and the children still in captivity." She died in April 2006, but she must have died with the Aboke girls' names in her prayers.

—Grace

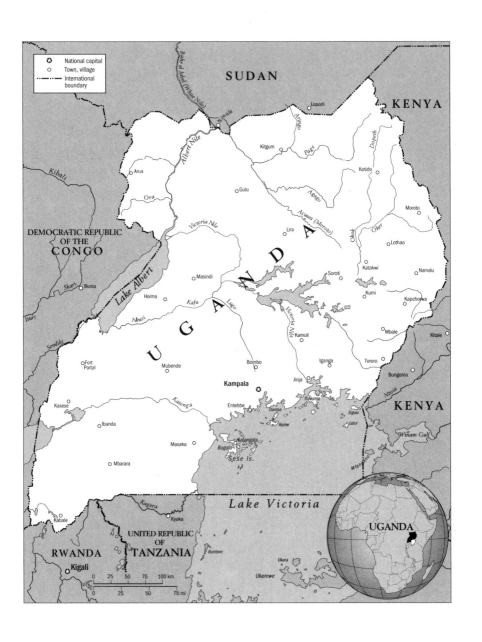

Contents

Contents

The Armies of Uganda
A Reference

In the following pages you will be confronted with a number of military and paramilitary forces and movements. These usually are referred to by acronym rather than name. Use this reference to avoid confusion.

FEDEMU   Federalist Democratic Movement of Uganda. A splinter group of the National Resistance Army of Yoweri Museveni against Milton Obote's government. Groups like the FEDEMU had an agenda of revenge and were responsible for some of the violence of the 1980s conflicts.

HSMF   Holy Spirit Mobile Force. The military arm of Alice Auma's Holy Spirit Movement (HSM). The HSMF fought with the goal of ending violence in Uganda and received its unorthodox tactics from spirits channeled by Auma.

LRA   Lord's Resistance Army. The rebel force of Joseph Kony that is now bringing suffering and death to northern

	Uganda and southern Sudan. Fighters for this army abducted Grace Akallo.
NRA	National Resistance Army. The guerrilla army of Yoweri Museveni in his bid to wrest power from Milton Obote and the Ugandan National Liberation Army.
PLO	Palestine Liberation Organization. A nationalist Islamic movement against Israeli control of the West Bank and Gaza and ultimately all of Palestine. Uganda's dictator Idi Amin Dada developed close ties with the PLO.
SPLA	Sudan People's Liberation Army. A nationalist resistance movement against the influence of Islam and efforts to introduce Arab culture in southern Sudan.
UNLA	Ugandan National Liberation Army. The army of Milton Obote that ultimately overthrew the government of Idi Amin Dada. The UNLA remained the dominant military force in Obote's government. Most UNLA soldiers were from the Acholi tribe and were accused of barbaric acts in civil strife against Yoweri Museveni and the National Resistance Army.
UPDA	Uganda People's Democratic Army. A paramilitary resistance force formed in Sudan by former members of the NRA after it was defeated and disbanded. Alice Auma said that she had been a prisoner of the UPDA.
UPDF	Uganda People's Defense Force. Regular army of the current regime in Uganda. Successor organization to the National Resistance Army (NRA) of Yoweri Museveni.
UPDCA	Uganda People's Democratic Christian Army. Joseph Kony's successor organization to the Holy Spirit Mobile Force (HSMF). Kony first called his military force the Lord's Army but changed the name when he rejected Alice Auma's Holy Spirit Tactics. The UPDCA, in turn, was the foundation for the Lord's Resistance Army (LRA).

Foreword

I stood outside and cried. It was not the kind of emotional response one might have to a touching scene in a movie. It was an overwhelming sadness and confusion. Little shoes, pieces of jewelry, journals and bones filled every corner of the church—the aftermath of a genocide that the world had either ignored or watched as if it were a foreign film without subtitles. They could see the emotion but they could not understand the subtext or the reasons it should matter. The dialogue was missing.

Rows and rows of human skulls lined the back walls of the church. If a skull had a distinct circular hole in it, the weapon that caused it was a club with a nail sticking out of it. If the skull had a clean line cut into it, it was caused by a machete. If the skull was simply crushed or cracked, that was most likely due to some kind of blunt object. The perpetrators had not used military weapons for the massacre. They had used the weapons of neighbors and farmers. For it was not a military force that had killed eight hundred thousand people in less than one hundred days. It was neighbors. It was colleagues, fellow workers and friends.

I sat across the table from a pastor who bore visible signs of physical abuse on his hands, his face, his arms. He had come under the cover of night to tell his story of persecution—the story of what life was like for him as a pastor of an underground church in China. Over the course of five days, I sat and listened to many testimonies, sifted through pictures and touched the mended hands of men who had been beaten and tortured. What was I to do with this kind of information?

I have always loved and found great purpose in a particular description of an artist: one whose primary position in this universe is to look at the world and describe it. A distiller of information. A prophet to a world full of busy and important people who need the "CliffsNotes" versions of how the world is and how it could be. Artists get to communicate what people should care about and why they should care. Artists get to tell stories. And it is in these stories that the cold and careless words and numbers, the building blocks of information, undergo a beautiful metamorphosis into meaning.

It is in the meaning of information that people find a point of connection and the context for understanding another person's circumstances. The artists behind the retelling of *Schindler's List* gave people reasons to reconsider the lives of Jewish families in the throes of Nazi Germany. We also cared to learn about the class system that allowed only the very rich aboard the Titanic a chance for survival when the ship began to sink.

These stories are the ones born out of artists who transform information so that we can find in the characters, both real and fictitious, glimpses of ourselves. If a story about a man defending his family from brutal force does not make us think about our own families—how we would defend them and the cruel things that could happen to our own children—and if we are not able to put ourselves in the place of the story's characters, then it is not a story but merely the careless documentation of an event.

We will not readily find ourselves in the numbers and words of information. That is why body counts and casualty figures fail to bring a true response or an impassioned cry for justice. That is why, when towers collapse in New York or a tidal wave hits Sri Lanka or an earthquake ravishes Cambodia or people make war in the Middle East, we detach and disengage as the numbers begin to whisk across the television screen.

The story of Grace Akallo is a hard one to read, mostly because she has been through things that we cannot even begin to have a context for understanding. In our psychoanalytical world, we do not see people like her as having a chance for anything close to a normal, unhaunted life. But the stories of people like Grace are invaluable because they are told in the right proportions.

Gary Haugen of International Justice Mission, an organization dedicated to saving girls from illegal prostitution and sexual slavery, said that the way to communicate the awful realities of girls in brothels is to give people 30 percent despair and 70 percent hope. He is right. Scripture tells us there are currents in motion that we will not be able to stop. Yet we see hope, and it allows us to push back against the effects of the Fall; it allows us to enter into what Dr. Paul Farmer calls "the long defeat." And there is at least 70 percent hope, because the Gospel is in these stories.

For certain, in the face of such brutal circumstances, we take hope in the fact that God is working out His glorious plan in our midst. But this hope sometimes loosens its grip when we consider the blackened heart of a man who revels in administering careless amounts of pain and affliction on another man. Or when we see the minds of men conjure up a schematic to desensitize children and turn them into ruthless, broken killers.

What does the Gospel say about children killing other children? What does the Gospel say about men systematically raping and torturing women? How do we tell these stories with gloriously disproportionate amounts of hope? Where is hope in the stories of the actions of men whose moral, social and cultural restraints have been lifted, who spend their days shedding the blood and drawing out the screams of other humans for pleasure? Is there really this much hope to speak of in the face of human bloodlust?

These stories are not the ones that end with reconciliation or with an overarching sense of redemption. Yet these are the stories that remind us why Jesus hung on a cross. The Gospel tells us that Jesus came so that the stories we tell will not end with torture and abuse. He died so we can believe in a God who truly raises people from the dead. Why? Because He knew that pastors in China and families in Rwanda and children in Uganda would need to believe in such a God more than anything. He knew that the last prayer a person utters before he or she comes to the end of mortality is "God, please be a God who raises people from the dead." By faith, they will wager their final breath on that being true.

And it *is* true.

So why do I care about these prophetic and artistic connections? Because this is a story that is still being written. Because in the beautiful and tragic land of Uganda, children are still being kidnapped and war is still raging and we are still doing so little, because we have not yet seen God or ourselves in the story of Uganda.

We are in the history of violence and corruption, in the blatant manipulation of spiritual things, in the wreckage of innocence lost and in the grip of mercy and strength evident in the lives of many child soldiers, even as the madness of war strives to snuff it out.

Dan Haseltine, Jars of Clay

Preface

The violence caused by the Lord's Resistance Army has daily brought death to northern and northeastern Uganda for two decades. The suffering of our people is incomparable. They have lost their children. They have lost their homes and their freedom, living now in refugee camps, lacking food and the ability to live a normal life.

We commend Faith and Grace for shining a powerful and compassionate light on the suffering of northern Uganda. Although their book illuminates the evil that was set in motion long before Grace Akallo was wrenched from the warmth and safety of St. Mary's, before Joseph Kony appeared in Acholiland to spill the blood of Ugandan children, and even before Archbishop Janani Luwum, my predecessor and hero of the faith, was martyred at the hands of Idi Amin, it is nevertheless *a story of hope!*

Over and over in the past few years, we have seen small rays of hope for an end to the war, only to have those hopes dashed. But heroic peacemakers such as the Acholi Leaders' Peace Forum and Mrs. Betty Bigombe have never given up. And advocates around the world have not stopped praying and fighting to bring peace and justice to the children of northern Uganda. Now, with the help of the regional government of South Sudan, another chance has come for the Ugandan government and the LRA to seek the way of peace and reconciliation and bring this war to an end.

There is hope for Uganda because the Christ, who was born, walked our world and died as a sacrifice, is alive. He is in control of our world and has plans, as the prophet Jeremiah said, to give Uganda "a hope and a future." Human events are not spinning out of control. God is with His people in the internally displaced people's (IDP) camps in Gulu, Kitgum, Lira and Katakwi districts. No one can shut Him out, even in the camps. As the tears and cries of our people continue to rise up to God for freedom, He is with them. Just as He delivered Grace from the rebels, He will deliver them all.

It is my hope and prayer that as you read *Girl Soldier*, you will see God walking with a young Acholi girl in her captivity, hear Him weeping for the deaths of His children and whispering in the hearts of thousands to raise up a movement for these children. It is my prayer that you will know God, who has caused *you* to take notice, pray and act on behalf of His children—not just because He loves them, but because He loves you.

Henry Orombi, Archbishop, Anglican Church of Uganda

Acknowledgments

Faith

I am grateful to Jane Campbell at Chosen Books for asking me to write a book about the children of northern Uganda, and for encouraging and challenging me in many ways. I am grateful, as well, to my amazing, beautiful and brave co-author, Grace Akallo, and I love how the Lord put "Faith" and "Grace" together to write this book.

Thanks to our editor, Paul Ingram, who smoothed over the rough spots, compensated for my grammatical memory lapses and helped me to trim my frequently long sentences; all the staff at Baker Publishing Group for their patience and assistance; my father and mother, Walter and Beatrice Hooper, who taught me to love the Lord (Dad is still loving Him here, but Mom is loving Him face-to-face); and Marilyn and Nancy, my big sisters and best friends. I must also thank my "soul sisters for Africa" — Pauline Hildebrandt (my Uganda missions connection), who convinced me to write this book; Fran Boyle, the intrepid and passionate

Sudan missionary; and Elizabeth Hankins, who selflessly helped and encouraged me in the midst of completing her own novel about southern Sudan.

> He is the image of the invisible God, the firstborn over all creation. For by him all things were created: things in heaven and on earth, visible and invisible, whether thrones or powers or rulers or authorities; all things were created by him and for him. He is before all things, and in him all things hold together. And he is the head of the body, the church; he is the beginning and the firstborn from among the dead, so that in everything he might have the supremacy.
>
> Colossians 1:15–18

Grace

First, I thank my publishers for their continuous support in the writing of this book. Special thanks goes to Jane Campbell, who was always there to listen and to give advice, and to editor Paul Ingram, who was very patient during the writing and editing of this book.

Thanks to the special people in my life who have helped me reach this stage of my education and have helped me pursue my dream. I thank Faith McDonnell for the idea of writing this book and finding the publisher for it. Thanks to Els De Temmerman, a journalist, the author of the Aboke girls' book and the founder of Rachele Rehabilitation Center. Els is responsible for my first years of college at Uganda Christian University. She showed me that I still had a future by sending me to college. She taught me how to be serious and hardworking, and she is the reason I majored in communications.

Thanks to Peggy Noll, who is most responsible for helping me learn how to write in English and write academically. Peggy has been a friend and mentor. She had confidence in me when I doubted myself and brought out the good in me. She gave me encouragement, constant guidance and tender loving care. She is a godsend who loves and cares about Uganda, and she is always smiling.

Thanks to Professor Stephen Noll, who is like a dad to me. He believes in me and encourages me to work hard. Without Professor Noll, Uganda Christian University would not be where it is now; he has transformed many lives. He was behind my coming to Gordon College.

My thanks goes to Mark, Daniel and Abigail Bartels, who made me feel that I have a family to turn to when I feel lonely. Mark is behind the sponsorship of my room and board at Gordon College.

Thanks to Professor Ben Bella, who taught me communications at Uganda Christian University and challenged me to work hard, to try to forget the past and to look toward the future.

Special thanks to my friend Henk Rossouw. He started the idea of writing a book with me, but we did not find a publisher. When I told him I was writing a book with someone else, he encouraged me. Henk is behind my first coming to America. He wrote the story about me, and people at Amnesty International read it in the *Chronicle of Higher Education*. He also helped me write and practice my speech for the first time I came to America.

I thank Jason at Uganda Christian University. He is like a brother to me; he encourages me and believes in me. I thank my friend Adeline from Uganda Christian University for her constant love. She helped me write my speech for the first time I was to stand in front of more than seven hundred people. I thank Rory Anderson, Amy Perodi and everyone at World Vision. They are working constantly to stop the war in northern Uganda by advocating for Uganda and giving psychosocial support to the children affected.

Thanks to the following people who are helping me financially with my college education: People from Uganda Partners, I can never say thank you enough. You are opening my future, you are turning people's lives around and you are giving them a future and a life to live for. God bless you. Tommy Hill and Camp Hill, thanks for your support financially and emotionally and for allowing me to be part of your home. I thank Kathleen Brown and John C. for welcoming me into their home. I was living with them when writing this book, and they encouraged me. John took some of the pictures for the book.

I thank Gordon College for admitting me. It is a blessing that I am here. Thanks to Silvio in the admissions office, who worked with me constantly when I was trying to get into Gordon College. I thank Arlyne Sargent for constant love and encouragement.

Thanks to Egaru Emmanuel and Paul Amoru. I thank all my friends who encourage and love me.

Last but not least, I thank my family: my parents, Etiau George and Molly Ajulo, who gave me life and sent me to school.

Introduction

Fifteen-year-old Grace Akallo was asleep in her boarding school dormitory room on October 10, 1996, the night the rebels came. Soldiers, most no older than her, swept through the St. Mary's College campus, threatening to burn alive any girls who didn't open their doors and surrender to them. Those who led Grace into the dark night had themselves been dragged away by other rebel soldiers, who had themselves been kidnapped. That's how the Lord's Resistance Army (LRA) of Joseph Kony gets its soldiers—more than thirty thousand of them.

But through a providential chain of events and circumstances, it was the abduction of Grace and 29 other girls that came to focus belated world attention on a humanitarian disaster that had already been unfolding for a decade in northern Uganda. For Grace was one of the "Aboke girls," missing schoolgirls who came to symbolize thousands of children who have been kidnapped, dehumanized and forced into a nightmare existence as soldiers and concubine "wives" for army commanders.

Grace's story and the story of Uganda are told in two voices in the coming pages. One voice is that of Faith McDonnell, an American researcher and writer who gives the historical context for the current crisis in Uganda and provides resources for prayer and activism. The other voice is that of Grace Akallo, who tells her own story of sinking into the abyss of hopelessness as an unwilling soldier in the Lord's Resistance Army and finding her way back through a miraculous and dangerous escape.

Within Uganda's violent history, the abductions of Acholi children and the forced relocation of more than 1.5 million Acholi to refugee camps have not often been on the front page. That the children have been the victims of unbelievable cruelty and forced to kill or be killed to serve the cause of a mystic spiritist could have become a footnote in the history of central eastern Africa.

But Grace Akallo's experiences illustrate why the people caught in a twenty-year civil war have not been and must not now be overlooked. The Aboke girls became important to the world because of the heroic tenacity of an Italian nun. The larger story of a generation of lost children commands attention because thousands of them are defying the inevitability of being kidnapped by the LRA. These defiant ones are the night commuter children.

The basic facts of this story are disturbing. On March 21, 1989, the LRA first attacked the town of Aboke and the boarding school located there. St. Mary's College is a Roman Catholic secondary school for girls mainly between the ages of thirteen and sixteen. In the first attack, rebels dragged away 10 girls and 33 others attached to the school and village and killed others indiscriminately. Headmistress Sister Rachele Fassera followed the rebels until she found herself caught in the middle of a firefight between the LRA force and a patrol of the government Uganda People's Defense Force (UPDF).

Eventually nine of the ten girls escaped. They had been forced to take up arms and fight for the LRA, and one was killed in a battle, years after her abduction.

By 1996, the security situation again degenerated. The rebels targeted civilians, and rumors circulated that St. Mary's College was again to be raided. Staff begged for more soldiers to protect them, but they were turned down unless they could provide transportation to bring soldiers to and from the school each day.

The raid came at 2:30 A.M. on October 10. Because the girls had been planning a celebration for National Independence Day, candy had been purchased and was taken by the rebel soldiers. Sister Rachele and two male teachers followed a trail of candy wrappers to the rebel camp. The nun convinced rebel leader Mariano Ocaya to set free the 139 girls from the school. Then a government helicopter gunship appeared and interrupted the negotiations. Ocaya later changed his mind and held back Grace and 29 other girls.

Sister Rachele and the parents of the remaining abducted children formed the Concerned Parents Association (CPA) to raise awareness of the abductions and work for the children to be returned. The story of the "Aboke girls" was broadcast by national and world media. Pope John Paul II condemned the abductions. Uganda's President Museveni wrote to United Nations Secretary General Kofi Annan about them. In the rebel camp, the girls found themselves the objects of particular anger. They didn't understand the reason—that their families had turned unwanted world scrutiny on the insurgency.

23

In June 1997 members of the CPA met with LRA commanders in Juba, Sudan. After first denying that they held the girls, the LRA offered to release them in exchange for a cease-fire. The Ugandan government rejected the proposal.

Five of the thirty girls died in captivity, at least three of them murdered brutally; all but two eventually made their escape by 2006.

The story of the Aboke girls mirrors that of the Acholi people of northern Uganda. The Acholi were Uganda's breadbasket farmers, an agricultural force spread across the savannah and hill country of three large districts of northern Uganda, south of the country's border with Sudan. That was before these farmers were targeted in the latest insurgency. Grace was a small girl, but she well remembers peaceful village life before the rise of Joseph Kony in 1986.

In that war, which has now stretched into the beginning of its third decade, Kony's LRA began attacking Acholi villages for food and children, filling the army with Acholi children abducted in these raids. The children undergo a systematic program of mind control in which they are starved and forced to break ties with their past by beating to death another person, often a brother, sister or playmate from home.

They are taught to assemble and disassemble automatic weapons and are sent out with Kony's promise that the ancient African spirits will protect them from harm in raids on villages and battles with soldiers. They are used as slave laborers, and girls serve the sexual lusts of older soldiers. Any rule infraction can mean being beaten to death or hacked into pieces with machetes as the others watch. The soldiers are led on forced marches until they die of dehydration and hunger.

24

Kony has ties to the Sudanese government and operates out of the region of South Sudan. But his army has mainly fought against unarmed Acholi.

Without the ability to protect scattered villages, and harboring a long-standing prejudice against the Acholi, Ugandan government leaders began relocating almost all of the 1.8 million Acholi into internally displaced persons (IDP) camps in the mid-1990s. There the tribal and family structure has broken down, and self-sufficient labor is a long-ago memory. Children of the camps remain vulnerable to abduction and have lost the protective family structure.

At this writing, the war continues, though peace talks have been attempted, and the fighting has less ferocity. Some Acholi are returning to their ancestral homes, and fewer children are at the shelter for night commuters. But the same problems continue, and new ones are arising. The Acholi still cry out to the international community for help to end the fighting and reestablish themselves in a new life. Not the least of the problems is how to reintegrate thousands of returning children who have seen and participated in unspeakable acts and are trained to do nothing except kill.

But this is not about the destruction of a hopeless people. It is about hope in the midst of despair and intervention by God in a hell where escape seems an impossible dream.

After visiting the country in 1910, a young Winston Churchill called Uganda "the Pearl of Africa" for its beauty and natural resources. But the true pearls of Uganda are the Ugandan people. Although it seems as if the world has forgotten the children of northern Uganda—that they have been, in the words of World Vision, "pitied and then ignored"—God has not forgotten them. To the Lord, the children of northern Uganda are more precious than the most expensive pearls.

God is working in Uganda, and the world's Christian community has a rare opportunity to live their faith in a dramatic way that has seldom been possible. The "girl soldier" Grace Akallo now fights to call the world to the difficult task of helping return emotional, physical and spiritual peace to the people of northern Uganda.

Grace Akallo (left) and U.S. Representative Christopher H. Smith (R-NJ) at a press conference on Capitol Hill. Grace was the featured speaker there on the same day of her testimony before Congress, April 26, 2006. (Photo by Faith McDonnell)

The Christian community is on the cutting edge of history that is being written today. It is the history of how God's people are answering His call to help save the children of northern Uganda. It is the history of how God's people are using the power and authority He has given them to change not just their own lives or their neighborhood but the world.

Pastors and politicians, poets and protestors, prophets and prayer warriors are working on behalf of the children of northern Uganda. God is committed to His Ugandan pearls. He is moving heaven and earth to rescue them, and He is moving hearts to make history for them.

Faith J. H. McDonnell

1

Buried Alive

"When death illuminates my way, there is
no sign of life."

The soil has become my blanket. *This bed is warm and com-fortable. Where am I? Maybe home? No, this is not home. It is quiet, only whispers of wind and the morning crickets. My foot hurts. I feel weak. What happened? I smell soil. This is strange.*

Slowly the bitter memories flow back to me. I am in Sudan, and I have been buried among the dead. Seven months after my capture, I am no longer myself.

When death illuminates my way, there is no sign of life. I have escaped death many times. Twice, I tried to shoot myself, and I would have succeeded if a fellow captive had not snatched away the rifle.

This time I have fainted from thirst. Thought to be another corpse, I was buried alive.

I dig myself out from under the loose dirt of the shallow grave. The grass and trees still stand burnt by the scorching sun. Even in the cold of the night, I resent the unfairness of the sun. The trees needed salvation like I do; I need salvation. Who would risk it? Who would face the unfair world for me?

My sense of direction slowly comes when I turn onto a path. I think of Paul, who was defeated by death. He fell with his eyes open. One moment I envy him, the next I am angry at my own spirit for not remaining in that grave. Instead I am still in this unfair world, where only darkness illuminates my life.

As I walk on, pricks of pain are all over my skin. There is no hope for me, but is there hope for Paul, lying there in the cold night and under the scorching sun at day? I am not sure. He lies there in the open, under some soil to cover his little, deprived body.

I continue walking. Walking has been the order of each day since I left home seven months ago. I did not know until later that the armed people who invaded my school on October 10, 1996, called themselves the Lord's Resistance Army. I only knew they broke all the windows and doors, tied the students and forced all of them out of the dormitory.

That night seems a very long time ago. Now I have become a skeleton that will not stay peacefully in its grave. Paul is better off. Why did I come back? Why?

It's a big question, and no witch can answer it. Even if I went to him, painting my body like a priest ready to celebrate the Eucharist, there would be no answer to my question.

A voice calls to me: "Who are you?" I look like a moving skeleton, and the person sounds afraid.

"It's me," I answer.

I hear someone jump from her position and run to another hidden figure nearby. They are close enough that I hear them whisper.

"That voice I know, but it can't be her."

"Maybe she is alive."

"Alive? We buried her. How come? I don't believe it. Call to her again. Maybe it is a mistake."

Yes, they are afraid of me. It is natural. I am a skeleton—no flesh, only sticky skin. Nothing in me qualifies as life.

"Are you alive?" a squeaking voice asks.

"Yes, I am."

"I told you she is alive."

"Come," a voice I recognize calls to me.

When I reach the two, they look at me like I have come from another planet. Maybe that is the truth. I can't really tell who I am anymore. And I don't have any clothes on me. I am just like the day I came from my mother's stomach. I am not ashamed at all. I walk to them, they give me something to cover my nakedness and they let me sleep near them.

2

Stolen in the Darkness

faith:

"Prolonged conflict has resulted in one of
the world's worst humanitarian crises."

A raw and savage grief fills the air in Uganda. The sadness in that grief is overlaid with an evil so irrational and unfiltered that it seems like the stuff of folk tales. It belongs to a nether world of ogres, monsters and demons of the night that come in the dark to snatch the innocent.

Since 1987, as many as fifty thousand children, almost all from the Acholi people of northern Uganda, have been violently abducted from their homes, refugee camps and schools. The mastermind behind these kidnappings is warlord Joseph Kony, the leader of a rebel force that calls itself the Lord's Resistance

Army (LRA). A former altar boy, he now refers to himself as a "spirit medium" and claims to have spiritual powers that protect him and his troops.

The LRA's stated purpose has been to overthrow the Ugandan government and raise up a state based upon Kony's twisted version of the Ten Commandments. Kony has promised that this would bring more power and justice to the Acholi people. But the war has brought only misery and destruction wherever the LRA goes.[1] This is particularly true among the children whom the LRA has exploited. While hard figures are impossible to verify, the Ugandan government and other sources estimate that most of Kony's force has been made up of abducted children.[2]

The LRA perpetuates a hideous cycle: Children abduct and kill children. These kidnapped children are brainwashed and transformed into killing machines. They are sent to attack villages, refugee camps and travelers on the roads. In these raids, the adults are often mutilated or killed, and more children are taken. The children who are not killed live in terror of torture, rape and death.

This is the story of one of those thousands of children. Grace Akallo—one of the "Aboke girls"—was wrenched from everything that made her life and from her loved ones and trained to be a killer in the Lord's Resistance Army. Her childhood faith in God was put to the test until she escaped and began an incredibly dangerous journey home.

Now a college student in the United States, Grace is willing to relive her heartbreaking and terrifying experiences in sharing her story because it is a story of God's faithfulness. It also is a story of 1.8 million war-brutalized people, most of whom live in exile.

31

A People Displaced

Prolonged conflict has resulted in one of the world's worst humanitarian crises. Most of the Acholi have been forced by the Ugandan government into squalid refugee camps. The camps are supposed to offer more security than they would have in their own homes on their own land. The Acholi have gone from being a self-supporting, thriving, industrious and proud people with an agriculture-based economy to being internally displaced persons (IDP). Around 80 percent of the internally displaced people are women and children. Some children have known no life outside the refugee camps. An average of one thousand children die each week in the camps.[3]

To avoid abduction by the LRA, many northern Ugandan children leave their homes in the camps and outlying rural areas every night before dark and walk as far as ten miles to such towns as Gulu, Kitgum and Lira. On any given night, forty thousand children, ranging from toddlers to teenagers, sleep in bus shelters, in churches, in hospital lobbies and on verandas. They rise at dawn to return home or, if they are fortunate, walk on to school. The children who make this perilous and exhausting journey have come to be called "night commuters."

To see into the lives of northern Uganda's night commuters is to be amazed by the resilience and resourcefulness of these children. Exhausted and afraid, they still manage to get to their nightly shelter. They do their best to study and complete schoolwork. But the anxiety that weighs on them day after day takes its toll on their spirits as much as sleeping night after night on a cold, hard floor or the ground takes its toll on their bodies.

"Pawns of Politics"

The northern Ugandan children, abductees and night commuters alike, have been described as "pawns of politics." In a report by that title by staff for the Christian humanitarian organization World Vision, the armed conflict in northern Uganda is described as "a tragic struggle for power involving children, who are used as pawns for military and political purposes. They are abused; they are manipulated; and by most, they are pitied, then ignored."[4] The report warns, "The welfare of northern Uganda's children has consistently been secondary to other political goals, even though children are the main victims of this conflict."[5]

Everyone seems to have failed these children—the Ugandan government and its military forces, the world community and even the worldwide Body of Christ.

The precious pearls of northern Uganda: children at play in an Awer IDP camp. (Photo by Sarita Hartz)

But God has not failed the children of northern Uganda. The account in this book is not a hopeless story about terrible tragedy in a remote country. It is not even an outraged cry for social justice. Scholarly briefing papers and reports by humanitarian organizations have covered these aspects of the story. But they have not told how God's heart of love and mercy has been at work.

3

Hope or No Hope

grace:
"Is it better if I go clinging to a little string of life?"

W ake up! It's time to go!" a voice screams. Yes, the day has begun in the usual tedious manner. I hear hands clap. That is the signal that we must begin walking. It is a never-ending walk. *When will this end, and why did I come back from that grave?* The only interesting thing in this life is the pain.

We set out in a single line. In the heat of the day, some people drop to their knees like Muslims kneeling to pray to Allah. People drop like rotten tomatoes. There is no strength, and their eyes turn and look up, as if pleading guilty before their forefathers. They will walk until it is time to give up and walk to another world.

We have spent two weeks in the wilderness with no water or food. Water is life—no water, no life. This is what I am seeing; now I have tested it. I am dry. Not a drop of urine. If I had some, maybe it would save my life.

"Where is your gun?" a commander asks.

"I don't know," I answer.

The commander, Oneko-la Poya, whose name means he killed a mad person, taunts me with insults: "I thought you were dead. Your mother must be pouring tears for you, or maybe she is a witch. People die, but you come back. Wait when we reach the base; we will see if you don't really die." This is scary. Maybe it is time to follow Paul and Acii into death. It serves me right. Why did I come back?

But I don't care about answering this question. Is it better if I go clinging to a little string of life? It will not help me. No hope.

Slowly, staggering like drunkards, a few of us manage to reach the base. I am one who made it, but I am a walking corpse, just waiting for my time to go back under that blanket of dirt.

"Attention. Left, right, left, right. *Nyuma geuka* — change steps. Who is missing? Count yourselves, beginning from here." The commanders walk around like heroes who have returned from some great war. I think of my great-grandfather. He went to fight in World War II and was a real hero, but he never came back to see the color of the soil again.

Oh, life is full of slopes, I think. *Now I am going through awful things that other people have had to pass through.*

"Attention, you. What are you thinking about?" Commander Oneko-la Poya bawls at me. "Remember, I am not through with you, you fool." He sneers at me as he continues to call out, "Left, right, left, right," to move the parade.

What might my mom be doing? Does she remember me? Dad?

I wonder what is going on at home. Maybe they think I am dead.

36

4

Fire of Martyrdom

faith:

"The testimony of God's past faithfulness in Uganda's history is comforting assurance."

Christians are in the majority in Uganda, and the Acholi are predominantly Christian. About half are Roman Catholic, and most of the rest are Protestant. They believe in the promise of eternal life with God, and as a result have been able to live through two violent decades in a country where violence has been all too common.

To understand the complexities of the situation at the source of the Nile River in Sudan and Uganda requires a trip back into history. Central to that story is the history of religious faith in Uganda, a struggle between Christianity, Islam and spiritism that is still going on.

Uganda's First Martyrs

With leg irons and yokes around their necks stringing them together, 32 young captives were forced to walk 37 miles to Namugongo.

Early in the trek, one was hacked to death. The next day, another was killed when he could no longer walk because of his swollen neck and feet. While such brutality is standard operating procedure for the Lord's Resistance Army, this incident took place one hundred years before Acholi children began to trudge through the bush under the guns of the LRA.

Whereas most of the northern Ugandan children taken by Kony's rebels survive their initial abduction and forced march, these young men were on a death march ordered by Mwanga. He was the *kabaka*, or king, of Buganda, the largest of Uganda's traditional kingdoms, which was a short distance south of where the Acholi are experiencing their tragedy today.

The captives who were not killed on the way to Namugongo spent seven more days in chains as an enormous pyre was prepared. On June 3, 1886, they were wrapped and bound in reed mats and laid side by side on the pyre. These former pages to Mwanga were burned alive for daring to refuse to compromise their faith and participate in the king's debauched lifestyle.

Even in their death, however, these brave young Ugandans thwarted the evil the king intended. They welcomed the privilege of dying as martyrs for Christ. Their attitude bewildered the executioners and soldiers who were ordered to kill them. One of the executioners later remarked that the prisoners acted as if they were going to a wedding and that the executioners were serving at the banquet.[1]

Certainly the martyrdom of these 32 and others that followed did not frighten away new converts or stamp out the flames of faith. Instead, their witness inspired and empowered the Church in Uganda. Today these young martyrs are revered, and their feast day is observed by Ugandan Roman Catholics and Protestants alike.

Channeling Evil

Throughout Uganda's history, violent rulers such as Mwanga of Buganda and brutal leaders such as Joseph Kony have emerged. The effect has been destructive. Some, such as Kony and his precursor Alice Auma Lakwena, the head of the Holy Spirit Mobile Force, have publicly declared themselves to be possessed by spirits. They have acted as mediums for those spirits. They may refer to the spirits that inspired them to commit atrocities and destroy the lives of vulnerable young children as holy, but the fruit of their possession says otherwise. They have "channeled" evil to steal, kill and destroy God's children in Uganda.

Mwanga and others like him have been responsible for the persecution and death of hundreds of Christians. These crimes pale in comparison to the horrors of Idi Amin Dada, who was president from 1971 to 1979. His regime tortured and killed from one hundred thousand to five hundred thousand (most sources say three hundred thousand) of his own people during his presidency. Amin and Mwanga did not describe themselves as spirit mediums, but their actions testify to who and what they were.

These leaders have created martyrs and produced mayhem, destabilizing Uganda economically, politically and spiritually. It would seem that these human beings have been the instruments of destruction for something beyond themselves that seeks to frustrate God's will for Africa. The current devastation of the Acholi by the Lord's Resistance Army and their debilitating refugee camp existence is not Satan's first attempt to block Africa's potential for greatness. The evil leaders share another similarity: God has brought good out of every evil during each of their reigns. God has never abandoned His children to face the trials brought upon Uganda by murderous kings and leaders. The testimony of God's past faithfulness in Uganda's history is comforting assurance. He is with the children of northern Uganda today.

Christianity amid Persecution

King Mwanga holds the notorious distinction of making the first government-executed martyrs in Uganda, during his reign from 1884 to 1903. He attempted to purge Christianity from his land. Catholic and Protestant missionaries had come to that part of central Africa not many years before, but Christianity was spreading across the land, particularly reaching young people, at the time of Mwanga's reign.

The Roman Catholic work centered in the White Fathers, as the Society of Missionaries of Africa was popularly known. This order was founded by Cardinal Charles Lavigerie, the archbishop of Algiers. Cardinal Lavigerie was an ardent foe of slavery, and he certainly would be a staunch defender of the children of northern Uganda were he alive today. The White Fathers established missions in the kingdom of Buganda in 1879. Fathers Siméon Lourdel and Léon Livinhac received permission to settle there from King Mutesa, Mwanga's father. By King Mutesa's order, the Christian faith was first preached only to members of his court.

Enough converts were baptized and shared the faith with others that Christianity soon threatened powerful witch doctors and Arab Muslims who operated the slave trade and promoted Islam. To protect their fledgling community, fathers Lourdel and Livinhac moved south of Lake Victoria with a few Christians whom they had bought out of slavery.[2]

In 1884, King Mutesa died, and his eighteen-year-old son Mwanga inherited the throne. At first it seemed that Mwanga would be a friend and possibly even a convert to Christianity. He began his reign by breaking with the old superstitions of traditional religion and elevating several Christians to high positions in his kingdom. Two of these young Christians, Joseph Mkasa Balikuddembe and Andrew Kagwa, encouraged the king to ask the White Fathers to return to the area. They did in July 1885.[3] The biography of Father Lourdel, *Planting the Faith in Darkest Africa*, notes that the priests' first audience with the king "was everything that could be desired." Mwanga was very friendly and made Father Lourdel promise that they would never leave Uganda again. He promised them freedom to teach and to make converts.

"If Mwanga remains in these dispositions," said Father Lourdel, "our catechumens[4] will no longer be obliged to come to us in secret, as of old."[5]

Purchasing Uganda with Blood

This mood did not last long, though. King Mwanga discovered that Christians in his court obeyed a "higher authority" than his own. They put loyalty to Christ above traditional loyalty to the king. The refusal of Christians to compromise their faith brought to light the offense of his own lifestyle. Mwanga was a pedophile accustomed to keeping young boys and men in his service so they would be freely available to him for sex.

Mwanga's *Katikiro* (prime minister) and witch doctors were jealous of the Christians. They and the Arabs, who feared Christianity's competition with Islam and the slave trade, convinced the young ruler that Ugandan Christians were in league with the missionaries to take over his throne for the Europeans. They insisted that the Christian pages and other members of the court who were converts should be executed.

The killing started in the fall of 1885 with the death of Anglican bishop James Hannington, missionary bishop of Eastern Equatorial Africa.

When news had come that this unknown bishop was coming to Uganda, the Arabs suggested that he was part of a "white invasion."[6] This caused great fear in the king. The Protestant missionaries asked the king for permission to send the mission boat to meet their bishop. The king sent two of his own men with the mission boat. If the men came back with a positive report, he said, he would then allow the bishop into Uganda. Tragically, a letter warning Bishop Hannington to wait for the king's permission to come never reached him. As he tried to enter Uganda from the Nile in the northeast, one thousand men intercepted and arrested him. He and his companions were captured by King Mwanga's men and tortured for a week. Before being put to death on October 29, 1885, Hannington's last words are reported to have been, "Tell the king that I die for Uganda. I have bought this road with my life."[7]

After this event, Mwanga's onetime close friend, Joseph Mkasa Balikuddembe, chief steward and leader of the pages, was the first Roman Catholic convert to be martyred.[8] Mkasa had been the favorite page of King Mutesa, and many assumed that he would eventually be made the *Katikiro*. Mkasa was a good teacher and mentor for the young pages. He was known for his generosity. He saved all of his money to redeem slaves and set them free. His friendship with Mwanga ended, though, when he confronted the king over the death of Bishop Hannington and over the king's sexual abuse of the pages. The Arabs and the pagan chiefs, who encouraged the king's pederasty, mocked Mwanga and tried to incite him to anger, saying he was no longer a king if he tolerated reproof from one of his subjects. So the king ordered Mkasa's execution.

Mkasa was beheaded and burned on November 15, 1885. According to accounts of the martyrs, Mwanga boasted, "After I've killed that one, all the others will be afraid and will abandon the religion of the priests."[9] Exactly the opposite happened: On the night of Mkasa's martyrdom, 12 catechumens were baptized, and 105 more were baptized the following week.[10]

One of the newly baptized was Charles Lwanga. Lwanga, said to be the handsomest man in the whole kingdom, took over as the head of the king's four hundred pages. He and other Christians began to instruct others who were interested in becoming Christians.

Six months after Mwanga killed Mkasa, he returned from hunting and summoned one of his young pages, Mwafu, the fourteen-year-old son of the *Katikiro*. He discovered that Mwafu was being instructed in the Christian faith by another young page, Denis Sebugwayo. For the first time, he realized that his court was full of Christians. Enraged, he killed Sebugwayo himself and instructed one of the Arabs to take Mwafu out and kill him, as well.[11] Then he ordered the palace compound to be sealed and guarded so that no one could escape.

The next day, May 26, 1886, he assembled all of the pages and separated the Christians from the others by telling those "who do not pray" to stand by him and "all who pray" to stand aside. Fifteen boys and young men, all under the age of 25, declared themselves as Christians. The chief executioner's son and one of the king's own bodyguards joined the Christian group. Another of the king's servants declared his faith and was immediately decapitated by the guards. The rest were given the chance to recant but stood firm. They were joined by two more soldiers, and Mwanga ordered that every Catholic and Protestant in the royal compound be put to death.

So it was that 32 Christians walked together toward Namugongo and martyrdom. As soon as he received news of the arrests, Father Lourdel hurried to the royal palace. He was just in time to say good-bye to his friends. The priest was overcome by the courage and joy the condemned converts showed on their way to martyrdom. When one of the Christian soldiers, James Buzabalayo, passed by, the grief-stricken Father Lourdel raised his hand to give him a last blessing. Buzabalayo then lifted his own bound hands and pointed up to show that he knew he was going to heaven.[12]

The East African Revival

Today, more than eight million Ugandans are Roman Catholic and more than seven million are Anglican. Every year on June 3, the faith of the Ugandan martyrs is celebrated at the site of their death, where both the Catholic and Anglican churches have constructed memorial shrines. The Roman Catholic shrine is built to look like an African hut with 22 pole-like supports that symbolize the 22 martyrs canonized by Rome. The Anglican site includes the Uganda Martyrs Seminary, associated with Uganda Christian University. The Anglican Church of Uganda believes that the faith of the seminarians will be strengthened by the testimony of those who died.

Less than half a century after the fire of martyrdom had scarred the land, a new fire blazed in Uganda—revival. In 1890 the White Fathers estimated that there were ten thousand to twelve thousand Catholics in Uganda. There were a similar number of Protestant Christians. The Church continued to grow during the years when Uganda was a British protectorate and after it achieved independence in 1962. But God knew that the Christians of Uganda were going to need something special in order to survive the years that lay ahead. That something was the East African revival.

The East African revival started when Joe Church, an English missionary doctor working in Rwanda, met with Simeoni Nsibambi, a Ugandan Anglican, on Namirembe Hill in 1929. Their encounter resulted in the transformation of lives and started a revival in East Africa that has never gone out. Christian scholar Michael Harper is quoted in *Christianity Today* as saying that the revival's effects "have been more lasting than almost any other revival in history" and that "its impact would become legendary."[13]

Another historian of the revival says it "was characterized by a deep remorse for sin, a desire for holiness and a close relationship with God, and treating other people with sincere love and honesty."[14] The fruit of the power-hungry and the possessed in Uganda has been seen in spilled blood and famine-racked lands. The fruit of Uganda's "revived" Church has also been tangible. Charles V. Taylor, an Australian Bible scholar and linguist who experienced the revival in Uganda firsthand, explains that there was a real difference between those whose spiritual lives had been revived and others, even other Christians: "Worldly business people would employ 'saved' East Africans in their homes and businesses, because they could completely trust them and rely on them to work hard."[15]

The transformation in the lives of the African Christians did not affect just their fellow Africans. The revival also had a deep impact on American and European missionaries who witnessed and then became part of what was happening. Many of these missionaries were totally transformed. Their preaching and teaching carried the power of God in a new way.

5

Safe Times with Grandpapa

grace:
> "For people in Uganda, the land is everything."

I was born into what is considered a very small family. My father had only three brothers. He was the second child of his father. In my culture, families used to have as many as fifteen children. The first child in my father's family was from another man, but my grandfather took care of him until he married and got his own house. My other two uncles were still living with their parents, even when they were grown. According to tradition, they would leave their father's house after they married.

Uganda is at the center of eastern Africa. It is a beautiful country and the source of the Nile River, which gives life to Egypt. Lake Victoria, the largest lake in the world, connects Uganda with Tanzania and Kenya as sisters sharing one umbilical cord from their mother. It is home to diverse animals, large and small. Beautiful birds sing beautiful songs to the Lord every morning. There are two seasons: a wet season when everything is lush and beautiful, and a dry season when trees and grasses dry up and water becomes hard to find. Crops must be grown when there is water to nourish them.

For people in Uganda, the land is everything. We live on the land. We survive because of the land. Raising crops and having cows and bulls for milk and to pull the plow and sheep for wool—these are very important things. The land belongs to the extended family, and no one wants to leave it. If people are homeless, as most people now are, then there is nothing else to take the place of the land. It is the source of hope.

A Place of Protection for Children

I was born in Kaberikole, a village in the northeast part of Uganda in the district of Soroti. The village I knew when I was a child was a special place. We children felt loved and taken care of. Life could be hard, so everyone looked after everyone else. Our hut was surrounded by our neighbors' huts, and children could run from one village to another without the fear of being kidnapped or killed by a stranger. Children walked about ten miles to school on lonely roads. No adult accompanied them, yet there was never news of any child being harmed. Someone nearby would have rushed to protect us. In my village, children were cared for by everyone.

Staple foods for the villagers were plantains, corn, millet and sorghum. Vegetables grown included beans, sweet potatoes and cassava. Cassava is a root vegetable that can be made into dumplings (cassava mixed with millet).

My father was not often around and did not help with the work, so we children helped my mother till and plant and care for the land. She raised millet and sorghum and cassava. What we didn't need for ourselves could be taken to the market and traded for anything else we wanted.

The market was at the center of the village and at the center of our social interaction. Everyone brought what they grew or made. What one family lacked in one kind of food or in cloth for clothing, another family made so that we could trade what we had for what we needed.

Until the Karamojong (cattle rustlers) came, we had cows and goats and bullocks to pull the plow. Wealth was figured by the amount of livestock a man had and the number of wives and children he could feed.

In the evening, families came together outside around a fire. Every home would light a fire at their compound to illuminate the night. This was the time when elders told stories to their children and grandchildren. Stories and lessons to be learned from them were taught from generation to generation. Youngsters were instructed so we could keep our treasured tradition alive and take our family on into the next generation.

So just as the land was very important to the Uganda of my childhood, so was the community and the family. These were the things that gave life meaning. No one could imagine that one day we might have to give up these very things. Who could have imagined that one day the children would no longer be safe by an evening fire next to their homes or in the village or on the road?

My grandfather was the son of a chief. He believed that he had power to control and protect people the way his father had. His father had been a respected man in the village because he was a chief. My grandfather's mother was the last of seven wives. Great-grandfather had authority in the village; nobody could stand before him and challenge anything he said. He was a hunter. He would take his male workers and dogs on a hunt, leaving in the morning and returning late in the evening. He would bring home a lot of meat when the sun had gone to her resting house. "I wished to go with him but he told me that I was young," my grandfather said. "I should grow first."

My grandfather was loved in his own family because his mother was the only woman who gave birth to children among all his father's seven wives. The other women were infertile. Children were regarded as a treasure, the wealth of a man. Someone was considered strong, powerful and rich depending upon how many wives and children he had. Grandfather's father had seven wives, but unfortunately only one gave him children.

My grandpapa loved to tell me stories. He would sit under the tree and would ask me to do him a favor. "Can you fetch me water?"

"Of course I can, if you promise to tell me stories tonight," I would answer. Then he would say, "Can you make a fire for today?" He was teasing me. He knew I was too young to make the evening fire. My two uncles and my mother would gather the children around the fire. I looked forward to the evenings.

I would do anything for my grandpapa. He was my best friend in the family. He could tell me stories and roast cassava for me. I remember when he told me about his father. He cleared his throat like someone who was going to speak to a big crowd, and then he would begin:

"Eeeh, my father was a strong man. He had seven wives, and only my mother had children with him. The others were all barren. He was a chief and was very rich and had a lot of cows. People came to our home to ask for help."

With pain in his voice he would end the story by saying, "My father died during World War II. I wish I knew where his bones are. I would go for them and give him a proper burial. He was a strong man. Maybe you will be like him, even though you are a girl." When he said that maybe I was going to be like his father, I would crawl toward him and give him a hug because I loved listening to the heroic stories. I especially liked it when my grandpa said I would be the next hero.

Change of Life

My grandpa—I have missed his love. He died after the day the Karamojong beat him. I remember that day. My mother moved like an antelope who was frightened of rousing a sleeping dog. Bad things happen at night. The village that had been peaceful, where people could stay outside late and walk lonely roads at night without fear, was under attack. Things changed with the coming of the Karamojong in 1986. Then they changed far more for everyone in Uganda with the coming of Joseph Kony.

6

A New Darkness Descends

faith:

"Janani Luwum stood up to an oppressive
leader and paid for it with his life."

The East African revival grew a Church that was able to endure the persecution and suffering that began with the coup staged by Idi Amin in 1971. Amin committed mass killings of his enemies, rival tribes and supporters of former president Milton Obote. Those who died included ordinary citizens, former and serving cabinet ministers, national supreme court justices, diplomats, scholars and educators, prominent clergy, senior bureaucrats, medical practitioners, bankers, tribal leaders, business executives, journalists and a number of foreigners.[1]

Throughout Amin's eight years of power, just as in the years of the Lord's Resistance Army killings to come, the Acholi, particularly the Christians, were a target. The fires of martyrdom would sweep through Uganda once again.

The Road of Suffering

What does a road of suffering look like? It all depends where that road happens to be. Christ carried His cross to Golgotha on such a road. There are many versions of the "Via Dolorosa" for those who walk in the steps of Jesus Christ. Often the road of suffering in Uganda has been strewn—literally marked—with the blood and bones of God's children. During the time of dictator Idi Amin, roads, hotels, the river Nile and even airport runways became places of great suffering and death.

A general and chief of staff in the Ugandan army, Amin seized power on January 25, 1971, while President Milton Obote was attending a conference outside the country. At first, Amin was welcomed by both Ugandans and the international community. He won the approval of both Great Britain and Israel with his promises to rid the country of corruption and introduce economic reforms. Amin also promised to disband President Obote's secret police, free all political prisoners and hold elections immediately to return the country to civilian rule.

The true nature of Amin's regime came to the surface as quickly as the bloated bodies of his victims rose to the surface of the Nile. Elections never took place while he was in power. Instead, Amin established the State Research Bureau, a death squad commissioned to hunt down and murder former president Obote's supporters and other enemies. The State Research Bureau was joined by the Public Safety Unit and the military police, bringing the number of men serving as security forces for Amin to eighteen thousand.[2] Much of Amin's interrogation of his enemies took place in the Nile Mansions Hotel, which became notorious as a torture chamber.[3] Reportedly, the number of corpses thrown into the Nile threatened to clog the intake ducts at a nearby dam.[4]

Amin decimated the ranks of Uganda's army with mass executions of officers and soldiers believed to be loyal to Obote. Some of the slain were soldiers who simply had not supported the coup. Reportedly, two-thirds of the army's nine thousand soldiers were executed during Amin's first year in power. In one instance, he killed 32 army officers by blowing up with dynamite the cell in which he had imprisoned them.[5]

In September 1972, Milton Obote tried to wrest power from Amin. Obote staged a military invasion that was supported by Acholi and Lango within the Ugandan army from his base in Tanzania. Obote's invasion failed, and Amin retaliated by bombing towns in Tanzania and purging his army of Acholi and Lango officers. Then he turned his wrath on the civilians of Uganda. One of his acts was to deport all Asians (most Indians and Pakistanis) from the country. Most of these people, third generation in Uganda, owned big businesses and were leaders in the trade and manufacturing sector. They also comprised a majority of Uganda's civil service. About seventy thousand Asians were forced to leave everything behind, and Amin allowed his soldiers to plunder the Asians' abandoned property. Severe economic upheaval and distress followed the departure of the Asians.[6]

Like Joseph Kony, Amin was frequently regarded as a madman, but a more helpful connection between them is their shared ties to Islamic regimes. The LRA has been supported in its destabilization of northern Uganda and southern Sudan by the National Islamic Front, now the National Congress Party within the Government of National Unity. Islamists in Khartoum have encouraged Kony and his rebels in part to retaliate against the Ugandan government's support of the Sudan People's Liberation Army (SPLA). This nationalist movement stood in armed resistance against the Islamization and Arabization of Sudan. After the British and Israelis distanced themselves from him, Amin reaffirmed his preference to Islam and received political and financial support from the Arab world from such countries as Libya, as well as from the Soviet Union.[7] Among all his titles, Amin added "Al-Hajji" to his name because he made the pilgrimage (hadj) to Mecca in 1970.[8] Amin had readings from the Koran broadcast every evening on Ugandan television. Although most of the world had not yet awakened to the threat of radical Islam in the 1970s, Uganda under Idi Amin was in danger of losing freedom and human rights and being forcibly changed into an Islamic state.

The most observable indication of Arab collaboration with Idi Amin was his connection to Palestine Liberation Organization (PLO) chairman Yasser Arafat. PLO training camps in Uganda schooled Amin's security forces and other military for killing hundreds of thousands of Ugandan Christians.[9] In spite of Amin's past relationship with Israel, including his training as a parachutist there,[10] Amin came to hate the Jews. In 1972, Amin sent a cable to the United Nations, congratulating the Black September terrorists for the murder of eleven Israeli athletes at the Munich Olympic Games. In the same cable he praised Hitler for destroying more than six million Jews.

In July 1976, when PLO-related terrorists hijacked a French airliner going from Tel Aviv to Paris, Amin permitted the plane to land at Uganda's Entebbe Airport. He tried to give the appearance of an honest negotiator between the terrorists and Israel, but Amin was concerned only with how he might be able to exploit the situation financially. One hundred of his own troops joined the terrorists in guarding the Jewish passengers and the flight crew (non-Jewish passengers had been released). The terrorists threatened that the next day, July 4, they would begin killing the passengers, one by one, unless Israel, Kenya and some other countries released jailed terrorists who had been captured in past actions.

Instead Israel conducted one of the most daring and brilliant hostage rescues of all time. Two hundred Israeli commandos, led by Lieutenant Colonel Yonatan Netanyahu, rescued the hostages and killed all of the terrorists. Only two hostages died in the rescue, and one elderly woman who was in a hospital at the time of the raid was murdered. The only commando killed was Colonel Netanyahu, the brother of the future prime minister of Israel.[11]

Humiliated and angered by the loss of ransom money, Amin executed air traffic controllers and civil aviation authorities, including those not even on duty during the raid.[12] He continued to commit atrocities of unbelievable dimensions until he was finally driven from power in 1979. He escaped justice in this world by fleeing to Libya and then Saudi Arabia.

Among the thousands of murders for which Amin was responsible, one stands out in its haunting similarity to the death of Joseph Mkasa at the hands of King Mwanga. Like Mkasa, Janani Luwum stood up to an oppressive leader and paid for it with his life.

The Subversive Archbishop

O God, by whose providence the blood of the martyrs is the seed of the Church: Grant that we who remember before you blessed

Janani, Archbishop and Martyr in Uganda, may, like him, be steadfast in our faith in Jesus Christ, to whom he gave obedience, even to death, and by his sacrifice brought forth a plentiful harvest; through Jesus Christ our Lord, who lives and reigns with you and the Holy Spirit, one God, for ever and ever.[13]

This prayer from the Anglican Communion speaks of Archbishop Janani Jakaliya Luwum, recognized as the first martyr of the second century of Christianity in Uganda. Archbishop Luwum died at the hands of Idi Amin in February 1977 because he dared to confront the regime with the evil of its repressive and violent actions. Besides reprising the nineteenth-century Ugandan violence, this execution foreshadowed the oppression of the Acholi people that is now taking place. Luwum was an Acholi, born in 1922 in the small village of Mucwini in Kitgum District of northern Uganda.

In 1948, Luwum gave his life to Christ through the East African revival movement. Throughout his ministry, he worked for both spiritual renewal and a strong, self-supporting Church in Uganda. One of his colleagues, Canon Kodwo Ankrah, a Ghanaian, extolled Luwum's vision and leadership: "Luwum made it abundantly clear that the Church itself must be educated to move away from its continued dependence on external support. . . . Luwum in his thinking was almost two decades ahead of many Church leaders in East Africa."[14]

Luwum was consecrated as the Anglican Communion's Bishop of Northern Uganda in 1969. Ironically, Amin, then chief of staff of the army, attended the open-air consecration with Prime Minister Obote.[15] As bishop of northern Uganda, Luwum gave a place of welcome and refuge to Sudanese fleeing from the conflict in southern Sudan. The archbishop of the Episcopal Church of Sudan was one of the refugees. Luwum also began implementing his vision for the Church as a key leader in civil society and as an economic support to the community in northern Uganda. He developed a modern church-dairy farm in Gulu and, with the support of German Lutheran Christians, acquired a lakeside guesthouse to generate income for the church and to help support the people of northern Uganda.

Luwum was as concerned for the spiritual welfare of his people as he was for their physical well-being. As a leader whose own Christian experience had been shaped by the East African revival, he stressed the importance of a personal relationship with the Lord of the Scriptures for both his flock and his clergy. He frequently led evangelistic missions and preached throughout the diocese. He identified, discipled and mentored young church leaders, including Henry Luke Orombi, who at this writing is archbishop of Uganda.[16]

Faith McDonnell (left) with the Rt. Reverend Peter Munde, bishop of Yambio; a young activist; the Rt. Reverend Enock Drati, bishop of Madi and West Nile; and the Rt. Reverend Henry Orombi, Archbishop, Anglican Church of Uganda. (Photo courtesy of Faith McDonnell)

Enthroned as archbishop in 1974, Luwum urged his church to reform in advance of the centenary celebration of Christianity in Uganda in 1977. It soon became clear, though, that God had placed Luwum in office to confront the evil enveloping Uganda under Amin. According to the Janani Luwum Trust in the United Kingdom, Luwum "exercised exceptional and courageous leadership when he opposed Idi Amin's regime of tyranny, gross human rights violations, and 'islamisation' agenda in Uganda."[17] Luwum warned that "the Church should not conform to the powers of darkness."[18]

Archbishop Luwum was criticized for maintaining an official relationship to the government because it seemed to give legitimacy to the murderous dictator. Luwum attended government functions in the hope of maintaining leverage with the regime. To his critics, Luwum replied, "I face daily being picked up by the soldiers. While the opportunity is there I preach the Gospel with all my might, and my conscience is clear before God that I have not sided with the present Government which is utterly self-seeking. I have been threatened many times. Whenever I have the opportunity, I have told the President the things the churches disapprove of."[19]

Luwum used his relatively strong influence on behalf of those who were being wrongfully arrested, detained without trial and killed. He often went personally to the office of the torture chamber known as the State Research Bureau to intercede for prisoners. Any accusations that Luwum had government sympathies were silenced for good in February 1977, when the archbishop's courageous confrontation of Amin finally resulted in his death.

A small group within the Ugandan military staged a rebellion in January of 1977. Although the rebellion was immediately crushed, with only seven men killed, Amin decided to use it to teach a lesson to anyone else who might think of dissenting. He massacred thousands, including the entire population of former president Obote's home village.

Soon after, the Church of Uganda used the occasion of the consecration of the bishop of West Ankole to condemn Amin. Before an audience that included many high government officials, in a sermon entitled "The Preciousness of Life," Bishop Festo Kivengere denounced the Ugandan government's abuse of the power given by God and the horrific human rights violations of which it was guilty. In response, the government raided Archbishop Luwum's house, supposedly looking for weapons, and attempted to depict the archbishop as an instigator of dissent and treason.

On February 8, 1977, the archbishop and most of the bishops of Uganda met to write a letter of protest to President Amin. Earlier, in 1976, Luwum had, together with Roman Catholic Cardinal Nsubuga and Muslim leader Sheikh Mufti, convened an ecumenical meeting to discuss the deterioration of Uganda and to request a meeting with Amin. Amin had responded with an angry reprimand to them for meeting together without his permission. This time, Archbishop Luwum went to see Amin and delivered the protest letter. He was accused of treason, the evidence being a document supposedly written by former president Obote that implicated the archbishop. Luwum and two Christian cabinet ministers were arrested and held for military trial on charges of treason.

On February 16, 1977, Amin summoned religious, government and military leaders to Kampala to condemn Luwum for "subversive acts." The archbishop and six other bishops were publicly arraigned in a sham trial for smuggling arms, but it was clear that it was Janani Luwum with whom Amin was concerned. As the church leaders were ordered to leave, one at a time, Archbishop Luwum said to Bishop Kivengere, "They are going to kill me. I am not afraid." He told the bishops not to be afraid, that he saw "God's hand in this."[20]

The details of Archbishop Luwum's death vary. The last that his friends saw of him, Luwum and the two cabinet members were being taken away in a Land Rover.[21] The next day, February 17, a government spokesperson claimed that Archbishop Luwum had died in a car accident. Later (to explain the bullet holes found in his body) the story was changed. Luwum had been shot while trying to escape from the soldiers taking him to detention.[22]

What is believed to have happened is that the archbishop was taken to the Nile Mansions Hotel for interrogation. When he refused to sign a confession, he was beaten, whipped and finally shot, possibly by Idi Amin himself, as he prayed for his tormentors. Then his body was driven over to give the appearance that he had been killed in a road accident. The body was placed in a sealed coffin and sent to his home village of Mucwini for burial. It was then that the coffin was opened and the bullet holes found.

In Kampala, a memorial service was held for Archbishop Luwum at a grave that had been prepared for him right next to the grave of martyred Bishop Hannington. Some 4,500 people attended the service. Another 10,000 attended a service for Archbishop Luwum in Nairobi.

Bishop Festo Kivengere learned that he was next to be arrested. He and his family fled to Kenya, along with the widow and orphans of Archbishop Luwum.

Contagious Courage

In June 1977, more than twenty-five thousand Ugandans gathered in Kampala to celebrate the centennial of the first preaching of the Gospel in Uganda. Many of the participants had fallen away from their faith but had come back to Christ as a result of seeing the courage of Archbishop Luwum and other Christians in the face of persecution and death. Since Amin's departure, the Church in Uganda has continued to grow, leading efforts to rebuild the devastated land. During Amin's rule, the Christian community actually increased from 52 percent to 70 percent of the population. When he returned from exile, Bishop Festo Kivengere declared, "Let there be no hate, let there be no revenge. We will rebuild our nation on God's love."[23]

7

Raid of the Cattle Thieves

grace:

"From then on I hated the Karamojong."

Grace, where are you?" my mother called. I jumped out of bed and ran outside with my eyes still closed. I suddenly was so scared that I could not even answer her. I didn't know what scared me, a dream or something that was very wrong. My mother's voice brought me to reality.

"Where are you? Come, let's go."

"I am here," I answered.

Her voice was shaking. I had never seen my mother in this state before. She was strong and courageous and daring. Once she killed a snake that was attacking someone. Everybody in the village admired her strength and dedication to bring up her four children after her husband left her for another woman. My mother was always the breadwinner. She would go hungry, but she would make sure her children were fed.

My parents met at a traditional dance. Young people would go to traditional dances at night to find a spouse. My father was still at school when he married my mother. He had come for a break. My mother was fifteen when they met and got married. She became pregnant with me and gave birth to me at age sixteen. Father was not at home when I was born, and it was my mother and grandparents that I knew well. After he finished his school, my father got another woman and left my mother to struggle with me, my brother, Alex, and my sisters, Sarah and Jessica.

Through all this responsibility, my mother was always calm and worked in her field from morning until the sun went down to rest. Then she would drop the hoe and put her children to bed. She used to say that it was a blessing from God to have health and land to till.

The night when she got me out of bed she was afraid. This was different, and something was terribly wrong. What it was I did not know. My mother pulled me from the dark place where I was hiding. She was in a rush.

"Pick up this bag, and let's move," she shouted. Children were not allowed to question elders, so I followed my mother. My brother carried cooking pans.

My grandfather's hut was opposite ours, so as we were passing, he called to my mother, "Ajulo, where are you going at this time of night with the children?"

"I told you that the Karamojong are coming, but you did not listen to me. I can't have my children here to be killed by the Karamojong." We had been hearing about Karamojong attacks, but they had not reached my village. The Karamojong are cattle rustlers who live in eastern Uganda. They believe that all cattle were given to them by God and that no one else is supposed to own cattle. They rustle cattle from the districts of Soroti, Katakwi,

Lira, Gulu, Kitgum and Kapchorwa. To hear that they were coming was such a shock to the people in my village.

Some people, like my grandfather, refused to accept the truth. They just called the Karamojong thieves and refused to hide from them. He said he would look for these thieves and fight them.

Since he refused to come with us, we left my grandfather in bed and went to warn the neighbors to run into hiding. They also did not believe my mum. "Go back to bed," our neighbor Omoto shouted from inside his house. "Where do you think you are going at this time of day?" We continued moving. At the time, I did not believe Mum either. I thought she was going mad, forcing us to walk at night when everybody else was in their beds. I was cold, and I thought my mother was punishing us. But I didn't resist.

We walked in silence. Only our feet could be heard and the singing crickets.

"Look," whispered my mother. "Those people thought I am going mad, but there are people hiding ahead."

At last we reached the next neighbor's home. It was crowded with many people. They whispered among themselves. Women were in the middle, and men surrounded them.

"Who is coming?" a man's voice whispered.

"I don't know," another answered.

"Who are you?" a voice called. It was Oboi, the owner of the home. I recognized his voice.

"It is me, Ajulo," my mother answered.

"Thank God. You scared us. Come sit with us," Oboi whispered. "Where is Grandpa?"

"He refused to come. He said he will wait for those thieves and fight them. My neighbors also refused to believe me. They think I am mad and told me to go back to bed."

"Who told you that the Karamojong are coming?" Oboi asked.

"My husband's family told me to inform Grandpa and go into hiding with the kids," she answered. "I didn't see the direction they took. By the time I came out, they had gone."

"Mama Stella told me. I also ignored her, but later I heard others talking about it," Oboi said.

The day dawned. There were few people in the market, few things sold. There was whispering everywhere. People were hurrying to go home. This was Saturday, market day for the week, the only day people left their homes to go and buy necessities. It was the day they took their goods to sell in exchange for what they needed, like salt and soap. Saturday was always a special day in my village and always busy and noisy. People called others to buy their things. Goats, cows and chickens bawled and screeched. People just sat chatting with each other about the harvest or when the rain would return so that they could begin cultivating.

But this Saturday was different. There was no chatting. The goats and cows escaped being butchered. Even the chickens did not leave their homes. Everyone moved quietly. Nobody wanted to tell their fears to their friends. They moved gracefully, as in meditation. The market was left empty and lonely by 4 P.M., though it usually would be full until 8 P.M.

Mum was not in a good mood when she returned from the market, yet she did not talk about the problem. She prepared dinner in a hurry. At 7 P.M. we were in bed. This was not our routine. There was no storytelling. Now I know why everyone felt so anxious. People were certain that the Karamojong would attack us this night.

"Do you think they will come today?" Oboi's question brought me back from my thoughts. The fire was flickering; someone could see us, but the group thought they would know better when someone was coming. Then people would have a chance to run away. People were tired of sitting outside. Oboi decided that women and children should squeeze into his hut. If anything happened, the men would get the women and children out and into hiding. Men were to sleep outside to protect the women, but this theory was later disproved.

Women and children went inside. I slept the moment I put my body onto the hard ground. I was tired and cold, so I didn't mind about the hard ground. I dreamed that my mum was screaming at me because I threw down my baby sister, and I was so scared that she was going to beat me. At that moment I was brought to reality. Someone screamed. I opened my eyes, and all was a big drama. The women were struggling to get out, but the door was not wide enough for everyone at once. Children were screaming, and women were cursing. Why had the men left them alone with the children?

At last when we were out of the hut, we saw that there was no male in the compound. They had all disappeared into the bush. There was shooting. I thought the Karamojong had surrounded us while we were sleeping. My mum told us to move with the people while she ran back to awaken my grandfather so he could run into hiding.

I felt unsafe when my mum left us, but, thank God, she did not delay.

"Where is Grandpa?" my brother asked.

"He still doesn't believe me," my mum replied.

"Leave him. After all, his days are over. Maybe he wants to die," said Lucy, Oboi's wife, as she walked in front of us.

We hid in a bush near the small forest. After about two hours, the awaited visitors arrived near our hiding place. They were completely naked. I had never seen a big person naked. I was used to seeing only my brother, so this was strange to me.

"Do you see that man? He is naked. Let's go near him and see," I told my brother, who was with me in the same hiding place. Mother had put us in a different hiding place from hers. This was good because we would have betrayed her with our curiosity. My brother and I moved near this man, but he ignored us because we were just children. He undressed all the women he got from their hiding places. He beat and raped some. It seemed like hell. My mum survived this. She was not found, so she was not undressed like the other women.

Finally the man cursed and told my brother and me to disappear from his face. Thank God, he did not kill anyone.

From then on I hated the Karamojong.

After the Karamojong left our village, people came back to their homes, but unfortunately some were missing. The Karamojong had killed them in their place of hiding. My grandfather was one of the missing. Tears rolled down my cheeks. I loved my grandpa. For three days there was no sign of him or even his body. For three days, I sat under a tree where we used to sit with my grandpa. I hated the Karamojong.

Then my grandpa crawled from his hiding place. He slowly reached the compound. It was a miracle; I shouted and ran to him. He did not hold me but he looked at me from the top of my hair to my toes. What had happened to Grandpa, I don't know. My mother came and took hold of Grandpa's hand and led him slowly to his hut. The Karamojong had beaten him. He no longer had the pride of the one I had treasured. His thoughts were far off. He spoke little and thought more. I had lost my grandpa.

8

Killing as the Spirit Leads

faith:

"The northern Uganda into which Alice
Auma was born was a deeply wounded
place."

In the beginning, there was Alice Auma. You could say that she created the heavens, the world inhabited by the spirit *Lakwena* and the earth — the world that would result from her Holy Spirit Movement. But instead of bringing order out of chaos, Auma brought chaos out of chaos. She set in motion conditions that would lead to horror for the children of northern Uganda.

Now there are Joseph Kony's "beasts," once-innocent boys and girls roaming the bush of northern Uganda and southern Sudan targeting other innocent young boys and girls and turning them into beasts. But before the beasts, there were the soldiers of Alice Auma's Holy Spirit Mobile Force. Before there was a monster who believed that the spirits directed him to bring about the purification of Uganda by blood, there was a woman who believed that the spirits directed her to bring about the end of war in Uganda by means of war. Her name was Alice Auma, but she became known as Alice Lakwena because *Lakwena* was the name of the spirit who possessed her.

What is there about Uganda that a small Acholi woman came to command an army intent on taking over the country? What can explain the monster who came after her, rising up fully grown from the bush to cut down people with less thought than one gives a banana one cuts from the tree? The alienation and marginalization of northern Uganda from the rest of Uganda plays a role in the discontent and resentment that enabled such demon seed to grow. Uganda's history is partly the story of growing sectional alienation between northern and southern parts of the country.

Uganda's history also traces the progress of cosmic war over the fate of the Pearl of Africa and the pearls of Uganda. There is something that seems bent on trying to thwart God's purposes for this nation. The evidence of evil at work in the land can be traced back to the flames of the bonfire where Charles Lwanga was martyred. Malevolent spiritual forces have been fed by bitterness over political and social alienation. And political and social alienation is the result of the prejudice and discrimination against the Acholi and other peoples, partly because their skin is darker than that of surrounding Africans. The northern Uganda into which Auma was born was a deeply wounded place. Many Acholi, and Alice in particular, felt scorned by the rest of Uganda.

There have always been ethnic divisions in Uganda, which came to be regionalized, north versus south. Wars and competition among tribes and ethnic groups existed before Africa was divided into colonies. Those conflicts in Uganda's history "have become the scars of the past," says Macleod Baker Ochola II, retired Anglican bishop of Kitgum Diocese and vice chairman of the Acholi Religious Leaders Peace Initiative (ARLPI).[1]

Just as there have been wars, there have always been opportunists who used the "divide and conquer" ideology to control others. That ideology worked well in Africa. Says Bishop Ochola, "The divisions between people groups that caused those scars made Africa much more susceptible to the violence of the slave trade and colonialism that left Africa depopulated and enslaved."[2]

Faith McDonnell (left) with the Rt. Reverend Macleod Baker Ochola II, retired Anglican bishop of Kitgum Diocese and vice chairman of the Acholi Religious Leaders Peace Initiative (ARLPI). Bishop Ochola came to Capitol Hill to testify before the House International Relations Subcommittee on Africa, Global Human Rights and International Operations. (Photo by Pauline Hildebrandt)

In Uganda, the north-south divide is between the Nilotic ethnic groups and the Bantu ethnic groups. Bishop Ochola, who is himself an Acholi from the Nilotic ethnic group, says that this division is at the root of decades of war in northern Uganda. It "is a product of bankrupt racial ideology of colonialism in Africa."[3] Europeans thought that the Bantu people were more "civilized" and intelligent because they looked more European. The Bantu had sharper noses and lighter skin color than the northern Nilotic peoples. In addition, their society in precolonial times had included monarchies. The Europeans loved that.

Of course, if the Europeans could have spoken to the late Bishop James Hannington or the White Fathers who witnessed the deaths of young Ugandan martyrs, they might have had some doubts about the civilized nature of King Mwanga. But by the time the British were making distinctions among Ugandan people groups that would affect the future development of those groups, their experience with monarchs was with a more pleasant and gracious descendant of the king who created so many martyrs.

Since the Bantu were judged to be more like the Europeans, it was thought that they would more likely benefit from education and business training. The British groomed the people of southern Uganda to govern the country. All the best educational institutions were created in the south. Southerners, particularly the Baganda, were given office jobs in the colonial civil service. Wealth-producing cash crops, such as coffee and tea, were introduced in the south.

The northern groups had no tradition of monarchy. Their society was divided into smaller groups, or chiefdoms, each headed by a *rwot*, or chief. Perhaps this type of society reminded the British of their traditional opponents, the Scots and Irish. Those ethnic groups also had clans and chiefdoms who made considerable trouble for the English. In any case, the tall, athletic northerners, with their darker skin and broader noses, were assumed to be better suited as soldiers and manual laborers.

"Their intellectual attributes were never considered," says Ochola.[4] The recruiting for the British colonial armed force, the King's African Rifles, was done primarily in the north.[5] Northerners were also recruited to work on the south's plantations.[6]

In her authoritative study of the war in northern Uganda, *Alice Lakwena and the Holy Spirits*, anthropologist Heike Behrend says that the division and hostility between ethnic groups was exacerbated by events in the postcolonial period. At the time Alice Auma was growing up, Uganda's atmosphere was one of violence and counter-violence. According to Behrend, "Whoever took over state power was not only able to gain wealth, but also to take revenge—against members of other ethnic groups or religions—as in times before the existence of the state."[7]

This explains why there was no reprieve from violence and bloodshed after the defeat of the ruthless Idi Amin in 1979. It was as if Amin's legacy, or curse, on Uganda was that evil would continue without him. The smell of war and death permeated the country, as group after group gained ascendancy, struck out at its enemies and then came crashing down. The soldiers of deposed leaders had to flee from the next leader who would seek to retaliate against them for wrongs they had committed. The Acholi were particularly vulnerable to this precarious situation. They had provided most of the soldiers since the colonial period.

After Amin's overthrow by rebel Ugandan soldiers and the Tanzanian army, a quick succession of interim presidencies ensued. Then national elections were held. The election was won by the former prime minister, Milton Obote. Disgruntled and suspicious supporters of other candidates accused Obote's supporters of fraud. The elections were hotly contested, but Obote ascended to power once again. Obote's election sowed more seeds of ethnic resentment. Division quickly turned to conflict when Obote was challenged by the president of Uganda, Yoweri Museveni, who retains control as this is written.

Museveni and his National Resistance Army (NRA) began a guerrilla war against Obote in southern and northwest Uganda. They established bases in the Luwero Triangle, an area north of Kampala. Obote countered the resistance with brutality. UNLA troops destroyed government buildings and homes and looted property in the areas controlled by Museveni. During this conflict, known as Operation Bonanza, Obote's troops, mostly Acholi and Lango, another northern Nilotic ethnic group, massacred as many as three hundred thousand civilians. Most of those killed were in the Baganda ethnic group, which was suspected of being sympathetic to the NRA.[8]

The Luwero massacre was another scar defacing Uganda. The Acholi suffered deep guilt for Acholi participation in the killing of so many innocent civilians. In addition, they sensed that they were the objects of hostility in other parts of Uganda. Many Acholi believe that their troubles now stem from the Museveni government's continuing bitterness toward them. They fear that many southerners believe they are getting what they deserve from the LRA. The government denies a policy of discrimination against the Acholi, but Acholi have to wonder as they languish in refugee camps and flee attacks by the LRA.

Whether or not the government believes that the Acholi should continue to be punished for the deaths, the Luwero massacre did wound Uganda deeply. It stirred another cycle of brutality that would first be felt by the Acholi at the hands of retaliating NRA and other troops from outside northern Uganda. Later, ironically, the Acholi felt the violence from their own people—even their own children—as the LRA turned against Acholi in a bizarre manifestation of self-hatred.

A Brief Reign for the Acholi

Although President Obote managed to put down the rebellion of Yoweri Museveni and the NRA in 1985, he was deposed for the second time by segments of his own army. This time the coup was carried out by Acholi officers in the UNLA who believed that their people were being exploited. They had to bear the brunt of all the fighting but never received the high-level promotions nor status awarded to Lango officers. The Acholi saw this as favoritism because Obote was from the Lango tribal group.[9]

Led by Lieutenant General Bazilio Olara Okello and General Tito Okello Lutwa, both Acholi, the UNLA took control of the government in July 1985. This was an exhilarating moment for the Acholi. For the first time, they had broken the alliance of other tribal groups and achieved national leadership.

The exhilaration did not last long, though. Only six months later, the Acholi suffered a humiliating defeat; the Okello government was overthrown in January 1986 by Museveni and the NRA. In its report "Northern Uganda: Understanding and Solving the Conflict," the International Crisis Group (ICG) explains that the defeat of the Acholi military and the Okellos by the NRA meant that, for the first time, both socioeconomic power and political power were solidly in the control of the south. The Acholi, the tribe of soldiers, had been defeated by southerners.[10]

Starting in about August 1986, the northerners reacted violently to the humiliating displacement of Tito Okello Lutwa by Museveni. Both civilians and former UNLA soldiers fought against southerners, perpetuating the cycle of violence and retaliation.[11]

Atrocities were committed by both sides in the conflict. Acholi civilians were abused severely. After their defeat by the NRA, Okello's Acholi UNLA forces fled back to the north with their guns. Some continued north into exile in Sudan and formed the Uganda People's Democratic Army (UPDA). Other soldiers tried to fit back into the agricultural society they had left, but they were no longer young peasant boys. The only life they had known was that of soldiers. That was their identity. Behrend says she was told that the soldiers "wanted the high life. . . . Like returned emigrant workers, . . . their return caused unrest and violence." Although they were Acholi, the returned UNLA soldiers had become strangers. They did not fit in Acholi society anymore.[12]

The most heartbroken strangers, now trying to find their way back into Acholi society, are the children of northern Uganda who have returned after being abducted, abused, brainwashed and forced to kill or be killed. Like the return of the soldiers of the UNLA, their return to their communities has often caused unrest and violence. In many cases, the trauma they have gone through has so damaged their psyche and changed their perception of who they are that it is almost impossible for them to "fit in" again. Grace Akallo, one of those children, faced these difficulties after her escape from the LRA. It is difficult for northern Ugandan children to go home again after they have been abducted and forced to be child soldiers.

In 1986, the idea of an army of brainwashed child soldiers was inconceivable. The human rights abuses felt most severely by the Acholi came from the Ugandan government's troops. The NRA failed to provide security for the Acholi in their problems with the returning UNLA soldiers. And both the NRA proper and splinter groups of soldiers were responsible for terrible violence themselves. One militia operating with the NRA, the Federalist Democratic Movement of Uganda (FEDEMU), killed forty civilians in Kitgum District. The massacre took place in August 1986 in Okello Lutwa's home village of Namokora. It was partly in retaliation for the UNLA killings in Luwero.[13]

Similar massacres of northern civilians took place over the next couple of years. The International Crisis Group (ICG) says there were even reports that the NRA buried a number of people alive during Operation North. Its "Gunga" Battalion raped men and women in front of their families to humiliate and degrade them, says the ICG report.[14] This brutal treatment caused many Acholi and others to believe that the NRA had purposely sent sadistic and uncontrolled thugs to northern Uganda, rather than the more disciplined forces of the NRA. It was viewed in the north as retaliation for the Luwero massacre and as a means of controlling them.[15]

Alice Auma wanted to heal the wounds of the Acholi. Both as a diviner and healer and as prophetess and leader of the Holy Spirit Movement (HSM), she desired to bring healing and redemption for past evils done to the Acholi people. When she began her journey as the chosen medium of the spirit "Lakwena," she believed this desire would soon be fulfilled.

That Old Religion

Auma was born in 1956 in Bungatira, a town near Gulu, and grew up as an Anglican. Her father, Severino Lukoya, was a catechist for the Church of Uganda.[16] Lukoya was also one of the founders of the Holy Spirit Movement. He helped advance the stories of Auma's encounters with spirits that gave credibility to her and the movement. His leadership of the HSM continued even after the movement's defeat by NRA forces and Auma's withdrawal to a refuge outside Kampala. It was strange behavior for an Anglican catechist.

Bishop Macleod Ochola observed that African cultures tend to define religious experience as integrated and holistic, "not private and segmented between sacred and secular or spiritual and non-spiritual as it is in the West."[17] The integration of faith into every part of life allows strong, spiritual maturity or else leads to spiritual disaster. The outcome depends on whether faith is grounded in the essential truths of Christianity and in the whole message of the Bible. Leaders often reject and manipulate the special truths, choosing certain Bible texts that can be interpreted as sanctioning their work.

Deeply committed and mature Christians in Africa move beyond many Western Christians in awareness of the intersection of the spiritual and material worlds. They don't discount the influence and power of "spirits" and of people who call on them. They see those spirits for the demonic reality they are. But their confidence is in God and their faith in the Lord Jesus Christ, not "jogi," or spirits.[18]

The Dinka in Sudan, with whom the Ugandan Acholi share Nilotic region beginnings, have similar traditional religious concepts. Dinka Christian hymns, of which there are thousands, integrate the old concept of the "evil jok" with the understanding that they are referring to Satan and his attempts to destroy people and the Church. They sing of the spiritual attacks of decades of control by radical Islamist regimes. In faith, Dinka Christians declare that the evil jok has been defeated by the cross of Jesus Christ and no longer has any power.

For others, however, Christian faith has not displaced traditional religion in their lives. Christian teachings only add new components of spirituality that they integrate into traditional religion. Such was the case with Alice Auma. As Alice Lakwena, she used an amalgamation of traditional Acholi religion and superficial elements of Christianity to mobilize her army against the government.

True Christians among the Dinka see that there are evil spirits whose origin is with Satan. They recognize that we can fight such power only by the power of the cross. In contrast, Alice tried to use spirits to fight evil spirits and bring healing to Uganda. She incorporated such Christian accoutrements as making the sign of the cross, holy water and prayer.

As a result, whereas previous fighting forces such as the UNLA had only secular, political goals in mind, the Holy Spirit Movement embarked on a spiritual crusade. Its members were persuaded by Auma that a spirit named Lakwena was calling them on God's behalf to bring cleansing and new leadership to Uganda. Without Auma, there would have been no Holy Spirit Movement. Probably without her there would have been no Lord's Resistance Army. Joseph Kony's claim to credibility was that he was Auma's spiritual successor, so it is unfortunate that Auma was not a prophet in the sense of being able to foresee the future. Had she seen what a Pandora's box of evil she was opening for the whole region, perhaps she would have been more circumspect about following her spirit guide. If she desired healing for Uganda, it did not come through her or Kony. She should have sought another way to bring healing to Uganda. Mixing traditional and Christian religions brought about the terrible nightmare endured by children such as Grace Akallo. Especially in the context of a military movement, that mix was not a good idea.

But the seductive call to the old ways is still too strong for people such as Auma to overcome, even were they to know what comes of playing with spirits. Lakwena and the other spirits are a respected tradition of Acholi culture. They provided guidance for the rudderless Auma and granted her the power, influence and stature for which she hungered.

Alice Becomes Lakwena

Auma's call came after many troubled years in her own life. The account of her past given to Behrend by Auma's mother,

Iberina Ayaa, is that Alice had a fairly normal childhood. The only traumatic incident she could remember was an encounter with a large snake when she was seven years old. This could be significant. In the legends of how prophets were called by spirits, a snake always plays a major role, according to Behrend. So Auma's early encounter with a snake provided authentication of her call to be a prophet and healer.[19]

Accounts differ about how many times Auma was married. Her first husband evidently was from Patiko, and her second was another spirit medium named Alex Okello.[20] Reports agree that she was unable to have children, which is a tragedy in Acholi culture. Both of Auma's marriages ended because she did not become pregnant.

In 1979, Auma returned to her father's home. Behrend's narrative tells that she began to work with a friend, buying and selling flour and using the proceeds to buy fish. They sold the fish in the town of Opit. Having failed at marriage and family life, Auma drifted into casual sexual relationships. She lived with a man from Lango for a time and had a reputation as a "loose woman."[21]

Everything changed for Auma in 1985. She converted to Catholicism. Then on May 25, she announced that she had been possessed by the spirit of a Christian Italian army officer who had died near the source of the Nile during World War I.[22] A manifestation of the coming of this spirit was that Auma seemed to go insane. She could neither hear nor speak. Her father, Lukoya, came to Opit, found her in this condition, and took her to eleven witch doctors. None could help her.[23] According to the legend that has grown around Alice Lakwena's life, the spirit led her to Paraa National Park. Her father accompanied her on this journey, which began to establish her reputation as a spirit medium. Now she acted as medium for a spirit named *Lakwena*, which is Acholi for "messenger." Auma became Alice Lakwena as she channeled the spirit of Lakwena.

The story of Auma and Lukoya's journey to Paraa, at the behest of Lakwena, became the official myth explaining the origin of the Holy Spirit Movement.[24] In Paraa, the Acholi already had areas of deep religious and cultural significance. The place where Lakwena led Auma was called Wang Kwar ("Red Eye") or Wang Jok ("Jok's Eye"). A shrine memorializing where a jok supposedly lived was on the spot, but it had been totally neglected during the civil war.

Another significance of the place had to do with the decimation of the wild animal population in the area at the hands of Idi Amin's soldiers. They had turned their machine guns on the animals as they were fleeing from the UNLA after Amin was deposed.[25] While in Paraa, Lakwena said that she held a dialogue with the animals and other forces of nature. In this dialogue, spirits and animals affirmed that nature desired rebellion and retaliation against all those who had injured the people and animals and caused great environmental damage. From this conviction, Alice Lakwena derived her authority for the battle.[26]

Other occurrences at Paraa helped equip Alice Lakwena for her office as a healer and diviner. She and her father heard complaints from the animals, the water and the mountain about the sin of the people. An account of this interaction was given to Behrend by Mike Ocan, a former member of the civilian wing of the HSM. In his version, the spirit Lakwena told all the animals that God had sent him to ask if it was they who were responsible for the war and bloodshed in Uganda. "The animals denied the blame, and the buffalo displayed a wound on his leg, and the hippopotamus displayed a wound on his arm. The crocodile said that they, the wild animals of the water, could not be guilty because they could not leave the water."[27]

Likewise, Lakwena told the waterfall that he was there to ask the water about sin and the violence of war. "And the water said: 'The people with two legs kill their brothers and throw the bodies into the water.'" The water then told Lakwena to "go and fight against the sinners" and said that it would provide holy water "to cleanse sins away and to heal sicknesses."[28] The mountain also named the evil that the people did and told Auma to fight against sinners.

During the final days of the forty that Auma and her father spent at Paraa receiving instructions from Lakwena and from nature, they were instructed to make a sacrifice in atonement for the sins of the people. The account continues, "After the offering, God said that there was a tribe in Uganda that was hated everywhere. This tribe was the Acholi. And God ordered that a lamb be offered, so that they should repent of their sins and put an end to the bloodshed in Acholi. The lamb was sacrificed."[29]

This judgment on the Acholi was a chilling portent of what the Holy Spirit Movement was to become as the Lord's Resistance Army. There was guilt on the heads of the Acholi for their role in the violence. There was also deep hurt in their hearts for the attitude of other ethnic groups in Uganda toward them. These were both legitimate burdens for the Acholi. It was the guilt that was magnified by Alice Auma. The indictment seemed to come not only from nature, but from God himself, saying that the Acholi were hated everywhere.

The path taken by Alice Auma to bring a solution for the guilt and self-hatred would result in bringing more guilt and more manifestations of self-hatred on the Acholi. And this path would result in the Acholi themselves being sacrificed, the ruinous sacrifice of the Lord's Resistance Army.

After the experience at Paraa, Auma became the spirit medium Alice Lakwena. She opened a temple in Obit where she channeled Lakwena. Auma did not appear to be very successful in healing people, according to Behrend. Nevertheless, the office of medium, diviner and healer gave her status and authority. She had lacked both as a barren woman. Behrend says, "The stigma of failing to conceive children can be turned to advantage in this way. The spirit forbids her to have children. No man, but a spirit now controls her body."[30]

Mobilizing the Holy Spirit Mobile Force

On August 6, 1986, Auma received a new message from Lakwena. He told her that it was time to stop her work of healing and divining. There was really no point in healing people when they were just going to be wounded or even killed in the war between the NRA and the Acholi. Lakwena directed Auma to raise an army. That army would do battle on behalf of the Acholi people. It would fight against evil and end the bloodshed in Uganda once and for all.

Lakwena directed Auma to call the army the "Holy Spirit Mobile Force" (HSMF). Later, members of the HSMF gave the following explanation of the creation of the army to local missionaries: "The good Lord who had sent Lakwena decided to change his work from that of a doctor to that of a military commander for one simple reason: It is useless to cure a man today only that he be killed the next day. It was his obligation to stop the bloodshed before continuing his work as a doctor."[31]

Iberina Ayaa, Auma's mother, told Behrend that after Auma received this directive from Lakwena, she was kidnapped by the UPDA and forced to work for them. This conflicts with the version of the Alice Lakwena legend told by her father. He said that the UPDA forces came to Opit, where Auma was still living and practicing divination, on August 17, eleven days after Lakwena's latest message. They attacked the railroad in Opit, and the locomotive engineer fled and hid in Auma's house. The UPDA shot at Auma, "but the bullets bounced off of her in a cloud of smoke." Lukoya said that when the UPDA troops saw this miracle, they asked Auma to lead them in battle against the Ugandan government.[32]

Unlike Kony's Lord's Resistance Army, which became a macabre children's crusade, the bulk of Auma's HSMF was comprised of ready-made, adult soldiers. Auma recruited soldiers from the former UNLA and from the UPDA, the resistance movement that formed in south Sudan after Okello Lutwa was deposed.

Holy Spirit Tactics

Auma started out with about eighty former UNLA soldiers. Later she was given charge of another 150 UPDA soldiers in the Kitgum area by the commander of the UPDA's 70th battalion.[33] She trained them in very complex and unusual battle strategies known as Holy Spirit Tactics. An example of Holy Spirit Tactics was that soldiers were forbidden to take cover when they were attacked. Instead, they were supposed to "face the enemy standing erect and with naked torso. Nor were they to remain silent, but to sing church hymns for 10, 15, 30 or 45 minutes, as directed by the spirit."[34]

Paradoxically, the Holy Spirit Movement was trying to conduct a war against war. Since for so long the Ugandan armed forces and their various leaders were responsible for causing such horror to the Ugandan people, Lakwena's desire was to build a different kind of army. He wanted an army that was not partisan to any tribe or ethnic group and had "moral strong behavior and God-fearing men."[35]

In order to more effectively wage this war against evil in Uganda, Lakwena needed help from other spirits. These spirits also came and possessed Auma, but Lakwena was the supreme commander and chairman of the HSMF. All the other spirits were subject to him. Auma would sit in a folding chair in the yard when the spirits took possession of her. At first each spirit identified itself by name, but eventually that practice was dropped as unnecessary. The soldiers learned the personalities of the various spirits. They could tell which spirit possessed Auma by the way it presented itself. Sometimes the spirits would come one right after another. The soldiers were never sure what or whom to expect. Spirits known as Wrong Element, Franko and Ching Pok were in charge of the A, B and C Companies of the HSMF. They, along with other spirits, took possession of Auma every morning and evening at seven o'clock. At these times they gave the troops instructions for battle, daily tasks and other such issues. They could also be summoned at other times if needed.[36]

Wrong Element identified itself as a spirit from the United States. This spirit led the HSMF medical training facility and was in charge of intelligence as well as A Company. Dr. Wrong Element, as he was addressed, was described by former HSMF members as having a very loud voice with a strong American accent. He liked to quarrel and scold and was very impolite. The soldiers were afraid of him.

Franko was a spirit from Zaire, also called Mzee, the Kiswahili term for "old man." He was described as having a friendly, wise nature. His job was the supply of food and other items needed by the troops. Franko was the commander of either B or C Company.

Whichever company was not commanded by Franko was commanded by Ching Pok, a spirit from China or Korea. Ching Pok was responsible for weapons and transportation. He was also responsible for the HSMF's stone grenades. The spirits revealed to Auma that these stone grenades, when thrown in combination with holy water before the advancing troops, would create what would amount to a force field around them, to protect them.[37]

Considering the use of Holy Spirit Tactics and reliance on such weapons as stone grenades, the HSMF did surprisingly well. In November of 1986, the HSMF moved against NRA units in Acholi. In several battles, the HSMF attacked the NRA, and the NRA attacked the camp of the HSMF. The NRA once more attacked the HSMF camp on November 26. That battle lasted only ten minutes, but the NRA lost 25 soldiers and large amounts of arms and ammunition. Only one HSMF soldier was killed, and a few were wounded.[38]

Outcomes such as this helped convince the people of Auma's spiritual powers. After this, many more people joined the movement, including UPDA soldiers, peasants, schoolchildren and students. At its strongest, the HSMF had seven thousand members.[39] Battles continued, and many Holy Spirit soldiers were killed or wounded. Lakwena directed the troops to rub their chests with shea nut butter oil. This "holy oil" was to ward off enemy's bullets.[40] If the directions given by the spirits did not protect soldiers, it was assumed they had sinned, not that the protections were ineffective.

Alice Auma really did want to heal the wounds of Uganda. The army she raised was meant to bring an end to bloodshed and war. She had a noble, if overly ambitious, goal. At least in the beginning, she also had moral, if bizarre, means for achieving her goal. The HSMF started out treating their enemies as human beings capable of reformation and, therefore, worthy of mercy. They treated prisoners with dignity and decency at the beginning. They even refrained from aiming at the enemy in battle. The soldiers of the HSMF were forbidden to kill early on. It was up to the spirits to direct their unaimed bullets to those who deserved death.[41]

The army Auma raised was meant to be a Christian army, bringing the Word of God to the people of Uganda and, eventually, to the world.[42] But the premise was all wrong: An amalgamation of Christianity and Acholi religion by a woman possessed by spirits, however often they might be called "holy," does not make something a work of God. As the magic spells, the holy oil and the stone grenades proved to be empty incantations, the ideal of keeping the HSMF free from killing and from evil had less and less influence.

The HSMF's last stand was the march on the capital city of Kampala in November 1987. Although they had moved far south of Acholi land to Jinja, which was only one hundred kilometers from Kampala, things had deteriorated pretty badly. The rule against aiming at the enemy was no longer observed, and the soldiers had become more desperate. In spite of their early victories, they now had come up against reality: The NRA had more soldiers and better weapons. They were losing more battles, and more of them were dying. They were discouraged and losing faith in Alice Auma.

With each defeat, more of Auma's soldiers returned home or surrendered to the Ugandan government. In the final battle on November 4, only 360 soldiers remained. They were thoroughly routed by the NRA, who set up camp at the exact spot where the

Holy Spirit soldiers planned to meet. The NRA ordered them to surrender, promising that they would not be killed. If they refused, the NRA would bomb them. This was the end for Alice Auma's Holy Spirit Mobile Force. Some soldiers answered the invitation to surrender. Others remained in hiding but did not fight and fled home. Auma and a few followers escaped into Kenya. The spirits left her.[43]

9

Buried Treasure
in the Abyss with the LRA

grace:

"Our silent fear had come true, and nothing could prepare me for it."

My mother encouraged me to go to school. She believed that it was only education that would give women a voice. She never got a chance to go to school because her parents believed that girls were only to learn to cook so they could please their husbands. Mother didn't believe that. She struggled to send me to school because she had seen that educated women were treated differently from uneducated women. She didn't want her daughters to end up like her.

Although he was educated, my father never wanted me to have my chance. He refused to help my mother pay my school fees.

But my uncles helped my mother. They never got a chance to complete high school, but they at least had learned to do business so they could sell their crops and small things like salt and soap in the village market.

I finished my primary school and was looking forward to joining high school when my uncles, who had loved me and supported me, crashed and died in a car accident. All my hopes were crushed with their bodies. I had nowhere to turn, and my mother had no money to continue supporting me.

Mother believed in God and prayed for me every day. She would say, "Grace, there is nothing impossible before God. You will go to school." I spent a whole year at home, helping my mother in the fields. We would get up very early, around 4 A.M., and go to the field to till the land until 11 A.M. Then my mother would send me to fetch water from the stream, which is about an hour's walk away. She would gather firewood and prepare some food for the family. Our main food was potio, made from beans and cornmeal. We would leave it boiling on the fire when we went back to the field. After having something to eat, I would go back with my mother to the fields to remove weeds from the plants until dinner. Then we went back home to have dinner and at last rest. Now it was just my mother who told us stories. After that we would pray and go to bed.

My father came once in a while because he was still married to my mother. She could not reject him because she was a woman and had no voice. It was on one of those visits that he came with one of the people he worked with and took me to the small town of Lira, where he was working. He took me to St. Mary's College, a girls' school in Aboke, a small village between Gulu and Lira.

St. Mary's College was in the middle of Aboke, a village that had no good roads. Sometimes the bridge that led to the school would collapse. The sisters would repair it and try to make it passable by car. The day I first stepped onto the grounds of the school, I knew it was the place I was meant to be. I started to pray hard to be accepted into the school because I was from the small village where school was not a priority. I was afraid my grades were not good enough for me to be accepted.

The school was quiet. Not a soul was lazing around the compound. All the students were in class, either flipping through the pages of their books or with their eyes fixed toward the front, listening to the voice of a teacher. I tried to peek in to see their teacher, but he was out of my sight.

I went to find out when the school's interviews would be. I smelled the gentle breeze that drifted through the rows of eucalyptus trees. The air was scented with the roses under the trees.

I thought this school was heaven compared to where I came from. There, trees were being destroyed. I love trees so much that at home I would spend my free time just climbing them.

"This is it, God. Let my dream come true. Please let them take me."

I very much wanted to be a lawyer. A neighbor had become a lawyer, and everyone in the village respected him. I come from a village where girls are not usually educated, and my dad had followed the custom. He didn't care whether I went to school. To make it worse, I was the firstborn, and my brother who came after me took all the attention. It was hard for a girl in my village to reach high school, so when I had this opportunity to attend St. Mary's College, it was like I had entered a new world.

The day they called me and told me that I was accepted as a student, I could not eat; my stomach was filled by the news. I suppressed my excitement because my stepmother was not happy about my going to school, especially since it was one of the best schools in the northern part of Uganda.

After two weeks of preparing, I left for my new school.

"This is your bed; you must make it every morning before going to class," said Angela, one of the student leaders. "Breakfast starts at 7 A.M. Be there always. I am also going to give you a place where you can sit every morning."

. I thought the people from St. Mary's were angels. Despite my being late, they spoke to me gently, showing me everything. Angela told me to go to her if I was having difficulty. I was late to report because my dad would not pay my school requirements. I learned later that one of his friends told him that if he did not send his children to school, he would suffer when the children grew up. But it was a pain for him to spend the money to send a girl to school.

I did not care. I was so excited to be at school and be loved as I was.

I prepared for my first class at St. Mary's. I unpacked the few belongings I came with. I had a few exercise books, one bed sheet and a bar of soap. My friends had a lot of things and were struggling to unpack. Some of their parents were there helping them. My mind flitted a little bit. I thought how lucky some people can be who were born so well-off. They had everything they needed for school while I had nearly nothing to unpack. But I was determined to be the best example for my village, so I quickly brushed the thought away. My first day I spent trying to think how I would respond to my teacher. My English was poor, and it was a big challenge.

"Good morning, class." A white woman's voice gently caressed my attention. "My name is Sister Rachele, and I am going to teach you biology and CRE," she said. CRE stood for classes in

Christian religion. It was the first time I had been in the class of a white person. This proved more challenging because I could not understand her. But after listening to her voice awhile, it was fine. I was now very sure that my dream had come true.

Our headmistresses showed great love, especially to some of us who had no love at home, where sometimes I was called a prostitute.

My elation of these eight months was stolen away from me on the night of October 10, 1996. I was well tucked into my comfortable, warm blankets. We had celebrated our Independence Day. During the day we had gone to church. There was so much joy that we were clapping our hands and shaking, swaying to and fro. After church, Sister Rachele, the deputy headmistress, and Sister Alba, the headmistress, put music on. This was a tradition for Sundays and holidays. This day music was played so the girls could dance and laugh. I was fifteen years old and ready to enter my "sweet sixteen" year. I was dreaming about the future, as many young people spend their time doing.

My happy dream came to an end when the rebels came with their torch fires. The torches shown brightly through our dormitory window. There had been no rumors of any attack. We had been taught to run into the bushes to hide if rebels came. Rumors of the rebels coming to abduct the girls would fly around the school like the announcement of a coming party. Before this day, there had been no rumors, so we all were surprised.

They started breaking windows, and they reached mine. I was sleeping like a baby when my window shattered on me. As if in a dream, I wrapped my blanket around my shaking body and dropped to the floor. I then rolled under the bed and found that one of my friends was already there. Then came the furious knock of rifle butts on our door.

"What is going on?" I asked her. She gave no answer, but the answer was so clear that even a deaf person could understand. My friend was shaking all over. For a moment I lay under the bed, hoping it was a dream, a bad nightmare.

"Open the door or we are going to throw this grenade in," screeched a voice from outside. The girls started running from one place to another, crying. Some called for their mothers. Some were trying to say, "Mary, mother of God . . . ," but they couldn't seem to finish the words. Our dormitory had turned into a dancing ground, with the music coming from outside. I got out from under the bed and tried to dress. (I was wearing a long nightdress.) When I looked out my window, my jaw dropped. There was no escape. The place was surrounded by hundreds of people, many of them children with bloodshot eyes.

"Jesus, help me," I said under my breath. It was the only thing I could think of that was easy to say. It became like a song in my head. I tried to put on my dress, but everything was chaos, and I just turned and ran to where other girls were running to and fro. The tips of the AK-47 were pointing in the window toward us. The voice outside was threatening to burn us. A girl opened the door because of fear of getting burned, and the Lord's Resistance Army dashed in.

Some of the rebels looked younger than I was. The young ones were rushing to find the leftover food we had kept. Within an hour, the rebels had tied up the girls in my dormitory. One hundred thirty-nine girls were forced into the pricking cold night. It felt unreal. No stars shone. Dawn was far off. No moon lit our way. Only dark clouds covered our fate.

This was a fear that no one had wanted to talk about. Our silent fear had come true, and nothing could prepare me for it.

10

Lakwena Seeks a New Home

faith:

> "Joseph Kony has definitely done his part
> to finish off the Acholi."

Alice Auma's defeat was not the end for the spirit Lakwena and his harm to the Acholi. After Auma fled to Kenya, her father, Severino Lukoya, claimed that he was now possessed by Lakwena and would carry on the mission. Like Auma, Lukoya manifested possession by many spirits in addition to Lakwena. He gathered about two thousand followers and focused his mission on healing and spreading the message of the spirits, rather than on fighting.[1]

Fighting was left to another would-be successor to Alice Auma, the man at the bottom of all the terror inflicted on the children of northern Uganda today. Joseph Kony claimed to be related to Auma. He also claimed to be both the next spirit medium for Lakwena and the next leader of the war against the government of Uganda.

Who is Joseph Kony? There are many opinions. The gut-level feeling of most people who know what Kony has done in Uganda and throughout the region is that he is a monster, a madman, a devil or all three. His followers seem to accord to him god-like status. At the very least, they consider him to be a prophet. Some dismiss his importance, in the same way some dismissed Idi Amin, as a lunatic or a buffoon, not to be taken seriously. But how can one not take seriously someone with the power of life and death over hundreds of thousands of people?

Unlike Auma and Severino Lukoya, Kony did not build an elaborate myth about his origins in order to establish his credibility and authenticity as a spirit medium, prophet or movement leader. Some of the few agreed-upon facts in the accounts of Kony attempt to paint a picture of his youth. But none of the glimpses into Kony's innocuous past explain his rise to power or subsequent actions.

Kony was born in the early 1960s in Odek, a village in eastern Gulu District.[2] He attended Odek primary school, where former classmates say he was a quiet boy who played football and loved dancing.[3] Raised Catholic, he served as an altar boy.[4] He is believed to have dropped out of high school, becoming a traditional healer.[5]

Kony's claim to be Auma's cousin did not stop him from showing contempt and hostility toward her while she was leading the HSMF. Nor did it stop him from terrorizing her father. Kony was a rival of both Auma and Lukoya. Former HSMF member Mike Ocan told anthropologist Heike Behrend that by early 1987 Kony was building up his own "Holy Spirit Movement," mostly recruiting former UPDA soldiers. Claims are made that Kony was initially a member of the HSMF and that he was a member of the UPDA before he founded his movement.[6] Ocan says that Kony and some of his followers once came to Opit. On that occasion, a reported spirit message from Lakwena tried to discourage Kony from maintaining his own movement against the NRA. Lakwena urged Kony to undergo a ritual of purification and join the HSMF. The spirit message ridiculed Kony for attempting to do something that he was not capable of doing. After hearing the message, Kony left the temple without saying a word.[7]

Kony's followers interviewed by Behrend said that he was deeply insulted by what Lakwena had said. He swore that he would never fight under the leadership of a woman. After that, there was no possibility that Kony and Auma might join forces.[8]

Lukoya also had a hostile encounter with Kony after he took over the HSMF. In August 1988, Lukoya sent a message to Kony, telling him that he wanted the HSMF to work in the Gulu area. Kony was based in Gulu District, so Lukoya was, in essence, challenging Kony's turf. Kony responded by sending some of his soldiers to abduct Lukoya.[9] He was beaten and held prisoner until May 1989, when he escaped.

Kony then renounced the spirits' role in warfare, at least in regard to the HSMF. According to Behrend, Kony sent a letter to Lukoya while he was a captive, threatening him if he should ever talk about spirits again. Kony's soldiers destroyed Lukoya's "yard," a small, round ritual center, and burned his Bible, staff and chair.[10] While Lukoya was in captivity, Kony came to see him. Kony declared that under his leadership, "no one would be possessed by spirits any more." He said it was the military, and not spirits, who led the people.[11]

Considering the history of the Lord's Resistance Army and the constant references to and acknowledgment of spirits by Kony and his followers, this is a puzzling statement. Kony's involvement with spirits started early in his career as leader of a rebel movement and continues as this is written. The first manifestation came when he was on leave from military duty and was working in the fields. In her book *Alice Lakwena and the Holy Spirits*, Heike Behrend quotes a report of this incident: "'Something strange came over him and people who were with him thought that he was possessed by demons.'" Kony was unable to speak for three days. During an attempted exorcism of the demons, a spirit message revealed that "he had been possessed by a good spirit sent by God."[12]

The spirit that possessed Joseph Kony identified itself as Juma Oris. This is quite odd because a man named Juma Oris, a government minister under Idi Amin, was alive at the time. The spirit Juma Oris became Kony's chief spirit and chairman, a role similar to that given to the spirit Lakwena by Auma. Other sources say that while Kony was contemplating joining Auma's HSMF he claimed to be possessed by Lakwena. Once he had broken off ties with Auma, he said that he was the spirit medium for Juma Oris.[13]

As Lakwena possessed Auma, Juma Oris possessed Kony. First a spirit message declared that "he had been sent by God to liberate humanity from disease and suffering." Also, as with Auma's spirit revelation, he added that healing was a waste of time as long as those who were healed were going to be killed in war. And so he was going to fight against all those who wanted to fight. He said that he had come "to teach people to follow God."[14]

In February 1987, Kony and his people kidnapped a UPDA division in Gulu District. Some of the captive soldiers decided to serve with him voluntarily. Others were kept as prisoners. Kony's soldiers trapped other units and added more troops to the movement. Kony had established his ongoing pattern of forcibly recruiting troops through attacks and kidnapping. At first, he was mostly capturing soldiers, but this was to change.

As early as the spring of 1988, the Lord's Army, as Kony's movement was then called, started attacking civilians. On Easter Monday, they attacked Lacor Hospital and the Sacred Heart School near Gulu. They took some 120 people, including female students from Sacred Heart, and stole medicines from the hospital. Kony's army had not yet evolved into the odious group of killers it was to become. They only kept the schoolgirls who chose voluntarily to stay with the movement. The others were allowed to purchase their own freedom by giving food to Kony's troops.[15]

Kony joined forces with a former UPDA commander, Odong Latek, along with 39 of his soldiers, in May 1988. Latek, who had refused to join Auma because of her unconventional tactics and "witchcraft," persuaded Kony to adopt conventional fighting strategies instead of Holy Spirit Tactics. At this point, Kony also changed the name of the movement to the "Uganda People's Democratic Christian Army" (UPDCA).[16]

Though he adopted conventional military tactics, he also claimed to be possessed by more and more spirits, of a variety that rivaled the claims of Alice Auma. Spirits included one known as Silli Sindi (from Sudan), Ing Chu and El wel Best (from China or Korea), Silver Koni (from Zaire), King Bruce Lee and Major Bianca (from the United States) and Jim Brickey (an African American from the United States). Behrend says that when a spirit

99

possessed him, "he wore a white kanzu (long robe) and a rosary around his neck—like Alice. Kony would sit in the yard on a metal chair holding a glass of water in his hand. He dipped a finger in the water and made the sign of the cross. Then he rose slowly, the expression on his face changed, and his eyes turned red."[17]

Kony allowed other spirit mediums to join his movement. Spirits that possessed some of his colleagues had such names as Bishop Janani Luwum and Bishop James Hannington, as well as two with the names of other early Ugandan martyrs, Kitzio and Charles Lwanga.[18] Other spirits were persons from the Old and New Testaments. In his own bizarre way, "Kony combated everything he considered pagan with greater severity than Alice had done, forcing an expansion of his Christian discourse through his radicalized structure of rejection," Behrend writes.[19]

A Terrorist of Civilians Emerges

Unlike Auma, Kony fought both the NRA and other resistance movements. He tolerated no competition. Neither would he tolerate betrayal from citizens. Betrayal could constitute collaboration with the NRA as informers or simply a lack of enthusiasm for Kony and his movement. Ostensibly Kony's movement was to fight on behalf of the Acholi against the government of Uganda. However, more and more of his victims were civilians. Most were Acholi citizens. Civilians were attacked and abducted to serve Kony as soldiers, porters or sex slaves. The excuses given involved some perceived betrayal of Kony, or no reason at all was apparent.

Kony has claimed that the Acholi should be killed for rejecting God's anointed leader (himself). "If the Acholi don't support us, they must be finished," he reportedly told one child soldier.[20] Kony has definitely done his part to finish off the Acholi.

In the first half of 1991, the NRA mounted a campaign against Kony's UPDCA. The World Bank had promised a large grant for reconstruction and development in northern Uganda, but a stipulation for receiving the grant was that there had to be peace and security.[21] The NRA crackdown in itself was very hard on the civilians—hauling people in for questioning, cordoning off sections of northern Uganda and dismissing aid workers—but it was devastating in the repercussions it caused from the UPDCA. The NRA insisted that civilians defend themselves against the rebels, but if they did they were regarded as traitors by the Kony troops. Civilians were forced to form bow-and-arrow groups to defend themselves against rebels with machine guns and other modern weapons.[22]

In Gulu District, Kony's troops encountered the bow-and-arrow brigade and retaliated against the citizenry with unspeakable violence. They kidnapped more than fifty men, women and children. Soldiers cut off the noses, ears and hands of some of them. With others they bored holes through the lips and padlocked their mouths shut. Others were hacked to pieces with pangas (machetes).[23] This brutality is confirmed by the Reverend Herb McMullan, an Episcopal priest and member of a church commission that met with Ugandan and Sudanese bishops in Uganda in 2000. The Rt. Reverend Enoch Drati, retired bishop of Madi/West Nile Diocese in the Anglican Church of Uganda, testified that he had received Ugandan and Sudanese refugees who had been maimed this way. McMullan wrote after hearing the testimony:

> They've held us down and pierced our lips and through the bloody, augured perforations in our forced-to-the-ground, struggling faces, forced the locking arm of padlocks which have no key, which when forced shut prevent the tortured ones from

speaking or eating but merely, instead, to advertise, like a traveling sandwich board, humiliation, intimidation, subjugation as a precursor to annihilation.[24]

At about the same time, in 1994, the name of Kony's movement changed again, to the Lord's Resistance Army (LRA). The National Islamic Front regime in Sudan began to support the LRA. The Sudanese are believed to have done this in part as retaliation against Ugandan President Museveni's support of the Sudan People's Liberation Army (SPLA). This opposition movement fought against forced Arabization and Islamization in southern Sudan and the Nuba Mountains. Groups such as Amnesty, Human Rights Watch, International Crisis Group and World Vision have all reported on the LRA's close ties to the Sudanese Islamist government. If it were not for the Sudanese Islamists' support, the LRA probably would not have been able to continue prosecuting their war on children for as many years as they have.

Collaborating with Khartoum in Killing

When the Sudanese government began backing Kony, the incongruity of Arab Islamists supporting a supposed "Christian" rebel movement was obvious. It served the Islamists' intent of forcing a hegemonic identity upon the country of Uganda. Bishop Macleod Ochola comments on this in his address "The Roots of Conflict." He said, "The Islamic Government of Sudan that believes in Shari'a [Islamic law] apparently saw no contradiction in supporting the LRA, a so-called Christian fundamentalist group, to fight the SPLA."[25]

Sudan did not see any contradiction in supporting the LRA because they knew it was no Christian fundamentalist group. The

Lord's Resistance Army still maintains some pretense of being a Christian group, and that designation is accepted by those who are fearful, suspicious or downright hostile toward Christianity. If the LRA were a true Christian movement, doing good things to advance the Kingdom of God in Uganda, the Sudanese government would have no part in it. Sudan promotes the LRA because it is a terrorist group that destabilizes the region and debilitates the civilian population in northern Uganda, in southern Sudan, in the Democratic Republic of the Congo and elsewhere. The LRA's hideous treatment of the African people fits the Sudanese Islamists' plans to destabilize that region of Africa and make it vulnerable to the spread of radical Islam. The relationship benefits both sides. The quid pro quo for the Sudanese support was general havoc in southern Sudan and LRA participation in military operations against the SPLA.

According to an Amnesty International report, "The Sudan Government provides the LRA with food, weapons and communications. It uses the LRA as a militia to attack the Sudan People's Liberation Army (SPLA), an armed opposition movement fighting the Sudan government."[26] The Amnesty report indicates that many of the human rights abuses described within it actually took place at military bases inside Sudan that were shared by Sudanese government and LRA troops. Amnesty declares, "It is within the power of the Sudan Government to prevent human rights abuses taking place and to ensure that abducted children are returned to Uganda."[27]

Much of the evidence linking the LRA and the government of Sudan has come from the LRA's young victims. Children returned from abduction have provided testimony on all aspects of the connection. A seventeen-year-old boy told Amnesty International what he saw when he was taken to Sudan by the LRA

103

in May 1996: "When I first arrived, the Sudanese soldiers identified a site where we could camp. Commanders sat together and exchanged ideas. Guns were brought in from Juba. The radio system was also provided by the Sudanese."[28]

The report said that children abducted in 1996 and 1997 told of seeing Sudanese soldiers providing arms and ammunition to the LRA. They delivered it in Sudanese army vehicles and helped to unload the trucks. The children reported that such weapons as AK-47 and G3 assault rifles, anti-tank weaponry, 81 mm and 82 mm mortars and land mines were all provided by the Sudanese Army.[29]

One boy abducted on January 1, 1977, was taught how to place land mines. He told the Amnesty International interviewer, "I was not trained in their names. I was shown how to use them. There are three different kinds. Small ones, which open like a mathematical set, for use against people. Then there are round ones, which are set off by 70–80 kilos—a bicycle will make them explode. And big ones, the size of a small washing basin, which are for heavy vehicles. There was Arabic writing on the mines. The Arabs also gave uniforms. I got one."[30]

The land mines have caused tragedy throughout northern Uganda and southern Sudan. In 1997, Bishop Ochola's wife, Winifred, became a statistic of those killed by land mines. "I felt like a tree split from top to bottom by lightning! I was suddenly robbed of a friend, a partner in ministry, a mother and above all, a comforter to me and those who were suffering all around us," Ochola said of his loss.[31]

11

"Shoot Her!"

grace:

"It was not yet time for me to die."

For twenty years, war has been no stranger to northern Uganda. Our capture could have happened on any day. Such irony that it happened on Independence Day, a day of celebration and singing in my country.

Led like slaves, we were taken toward a life of torment. We left our independence behind. We moved the whole night. Sister Rachele had hidden behind the banana plantation because she feared the rebels would force her to tell where the other girls were hiding. There were two dormitories. The rebels had attacked the one for the young students. The older girls were saved because dried corn was spread under the porch of their dormitory, giving them places to hide.

Sister Rachele tracked our footprints and caught up with us. When she arrived, her eyes were bloodshot, for she had been crying all the time she looked for us. When I saw her, the tears that had been hiding behind my eyelids freely dropped. It was a relief to see someone whom I believed would do something.

"You are crying? You are not leaving here. We will either rape you or kill you," our guards told us when Sister Rachele first came into sight. She now walked by our side for the whole day, pleading with the commander, Lagira, for our release.

At 6 p.m., sitting under the banana plantation in a deserted home, we had hopes of going back to the school.

Something is going on here, I thought. *Why are they selecting people?*

"Get up and join the other group," someone told me. My wandering mind was jolted back to reality.

An hour later, we had been divided into two groups. One group of 109 girls was released to Sister Rachele. I was one of the thirty Lagira decided to keep. That night we were packed like pigs into a tiny round hut, which barely had space for a single bed. We had nothing to eat. Most of us were wearing only our thin nightdresses. With no shoes or slippers, our legs were muddy and already blistered. There was no sleep for us that night, only tears—rivers of tears. I had never prayed that way before. I repented of my sins and promised God that I would never turn my back on Him if I survived. My faith strengthened after my prayers. I believed God would rescue me, and that faith kept me alive.

A twelve-year-old girl tried to escape two weeks after our capture. Her head was smashed. This was scary. The thought of escape left me immediately. I had never seen this before. While the memory of the girl's murder was still fresh, the commander called the thirty Aboke girls.

"You are each going to be beaten one hundred strokes to teach you a lesson," Lagira announced when we reached where he was seated. It was not a lie. The sticks were lying neatly waiting for us, and the young soldiers were ready for action. We were beaten until I saw another world.

Survival here will be hard, I thought as I drifted back to my world of grief.

We wandered through Gulu and Kitgum districts, looting, killing and abducting more children. I got sick and weak and had to drag my feet, but I tried to summon all my strength. One day there was a fight between Ugandan solders and the rebels. I dropped the baggage I was given to carry, a tent and a cooking pot. These were very important to the rebels. That I had left these things behind was not discovered until a week later when the rain was threatening to pour, when the commander, BM Oyet, called his wife and asked her where the tent was.

"You gave it to one of the Aboke girls," the wife answered. That was how they identified us from the others.

"Who is it, and where is she?" he asked her.

"Grace," she answered.

"Grace, I want the tent," he called to me.

My legs were dancing because I thought this was my last day to live. I told my friend Agnes, one of the Aboke, to pray for my spirit. I walked slowly, trying to take in as much air as I could for the last time on earth.

"I will," she said, her voice hoarse with grief.

I prayed under my breath because I didn't want the man to hear me pray, "Please take my spirit into Your hand and don't let me feel the pain." After that prayer, my head just started singing, *Jesus, help me*. I did not know whether I was asking Jesus to help me live or help me die and take my spirit. Everybody who lived under this man was called to witness the killing. That is what they usually do when they are killing someone. A bunch of sticks were lying there waiting for me.

"Lie down," BM Oyet shrieked at me the moment I reached where he was seated, and everyone looked on like I was a goat taken for slaughter for Christmas. I went down, singing for help from Jesus. It was the only name I could call at that moment. My mother could not help me. Nobody else could help except Jesus.

"Get up." BM's voice woke me up from my thoughts after I had been lying there for what seemed like a thousand years, waiting to be slaughtered. When I lifted my head, the commander was shifting uneasily in his chair like something was biting him.

"Shoot her!" he screamed at one of his escorts. This was unusual. These people usually don't shoot anyone except when they are fighting against the Ugandan army. As the boy was preparing to shoot, BM Oyet screamed again at the boy not to shoot me. This came as a surprise to me and to the others who were standing around watching.

He then warned me, "If you lose anything else, even a needle, know that you are dead. Disappear from my sight before I change my mind. You are lucky that I am not in the mood to kill today."

After about a month, the rebels divided the Aboke girls into two groups. I was among the first group, which was marched farther north a week later, following the flow of the Nile River into Sudan.

Barefoot, I tried to ease the blisters on my rotting feet by wrapping them with leaves. I was feverish, I felt nauseous and I often had diarrhea. I was too weak to walk fast. But even the hardened rebels were not spared. Those who slackened their pace were promised death by bayonet, so that they could "rest forever."

After four days and nights on the march, starving and aching for water, we reached the main training camp in Sudan, where the Muslim government in Khartoum supported the Lord's Resistance Army with weapons and uniforms.

It wasn't that the rebels were interested in becoming Muslims. For the most part they weren't religious except for Kony, who believed a mix of Christianity and a mystical sort of spiritism. But it was in the best interests of the Muslims to help the Ugandan rebels, and the Ugandan rebels got good weapons and supplies by helping the Sudanese.

Our base was in Aruu, a village in southern Sudan. In that general area an insurgent force led by John Garang was fighting against the Muslim government. The LRA was treated like a hired mercenary force to attack Garang's rebels so that they couldn't assault Sudan's army in force. The Islamic government at Khartoum was very well funded, but they didn't want to fight their enemy if they could have us do it for the guns, ammunition and uniforms they had at hand.

The place had the smell of death. Before I went far into the camp, I knew there was great trouble, but I had given up. I had no hope of escape, and home was many miles away. I was in a strange land with the most heartless people ever known.

We had to assemble before the leader of the rebel movement, Joseph Kony, on the parade ground. "Aboke girls should forget about going back to Uganda," Kony said. "They should be trained to fight."

A week later, the commanders gave us AK-47 assault rifles and taught us how to dismantle, clean and assemble them. "Hunger will teach you how to shoot," they said.

Kony distributed us among his commanders. I was given to a man older than my father. His eyes were so hard that my sweat made a pool.

"Remove your clothes," he ordered. I was too scared to move. How could this man do this to me? I wanted to shout, "Who can help me? God, help me." He seized me and forced me to bed. I felt like a thorn was in my skin as my innocence was destroyed.

They were right. Hunger taught me how to fight. We raided villages, looking for food and water. Our commanders, our so-called husbands, provided nothing. We were forced to eat lizards, rats, wild fruits, leaves, roots and soil. We walked about three miles from the camp to look for water. We had to dig in the sand with our fingers and then wait for hours for moisture to seep out. Some could not wait. The path to the water place was strewn with corpses.

Finally I was so tired and sick that I could not do what they asked any longer. My sight went black, and I fell down while a group was out looking for food. My friend Paul also fell nearby. He died that day. I didn't, but they thought I had. I was buried in a shallow grave. After I awoke and dug myself out, I followed the others until I reached them. They thought I was a ghost. I don't know why I went back to them, except that I didn't care any longer.

Not many days after I arrived back at the training camp, I was summoned by a man who had my life in his hands. But at that point I was beyond fear.

"Where is your bag?" The voice brought me back from my secret heart cry. Maybe it was not a heart cry but a heart from which blood was trickling down, though the blood couldn't be seen by an eye.

"I don't know. Somebody took it," I answered him.

"What? The master wants the share that you brought."

Since the day I was grabbed, brought here and taught how to fight, it had been understood that we must give something to Kony when we came back from our raids. I had looted groundnuts and sorghum, but the bag was taken from me while I was lying covered with dirt in my deep sleep. I loved that sweet, deep sleep. I did not have to deal with the men and their red, bloodshot eyes.

But now everyone was giving except me. The man promised to kill me later.

Here I was, this man threatening to kill me, and I didn't care. If he didn't kill me, I had to go back to that ugly man with his dreadful eyes. Why did I come back? Paul was right to remain in the scorching sun. God help me, what was going to happen to me? Would I die in this land and be left in the cold?

"You can go now, but Grace should remain," Commander Oneko-la Poya ordered the others.

By this time, I was scared in my heart. I thought my time had come. How did Jesus feel that day, when He was about to be crucified? I don't know. Death is scary, even for a walking skeleton with rotting feet.

"Come here, you dupe thing. Lie down. I want to show you how to be a strong soldier, so that you don't pretend to be dead," he said.

"No, please don't beat me. Forgive me. I promise I will follow your commands." I pleaded with him, but he did not listen to me. Through the pain in my skin, I could not cry anymore. I felt the earth rotating. Maybe I was going to die this time. "Jesus," I said, "take my spirit."

He finished beating me. "Get up. Remember, the next time you don't follow the rules you will be dead." As a faint sound, I heard him say this and order me to go to my unit. My husband might be waiting for me. That man who forced me to go to bed with him and is older than my dad was considered my husband. I didn't know what he would tell me now that I had come with nothing from the raid. He might be the one to kill me that day.

Slowly I walked back. Lakati, my husband, was seated under the tree like a *jaja*, or grandfather, waiting to tell me stories of his past. Now I might also die in the wild, like my grandfather. He was a great man, according to his son. What about me? I would die, and nobody would remember me, I thought.

"Where have you been, you lazy woman? People have all come back early." His voice sounded rough, like an elephant's bellow. This did not take me by surprise. I knew he would grunt like an angry lion. "What happened to you? Where is your gun? What have you brought from the raid?"

"*Aloko dong koo.* I cannot talk anymore," I whispered. I had forgotten about the gun. During my sweet sleep, whoever had taken my groundnuts had also taken my gun.

"Come here, you swine," he ordered. "You only know how to eat."

I had no voice. He was a major general and had the right to do anything to me. Not a fly hung around him. He had beaten me before, and nobody lifted a finger to stop him.

"Lawang-tek ["strong-eyed"], go get me that club over there. I am tired of this fool."

This is it. If I survive this one, I will survive, and I will probably die at an old age. O God, has my time come? Don't You think I should see my parents again and say good-bye to them? Then I will be happy to come. But if it is time, please let me not feel the pain of death. I am so scared. Please, Jesus, hold my hand. Let me look just at You, not at the death that I am facing now. Protect my friends; let them go tell my parents what happened to me so that they will not keep waiting or hope for my return. Keep my mother and give her a heart to forgive this crime.

"Get up," my husband ordered. "You are lucky the spirit has stopped me from spilling your blood. This spirit is a spirit of peace," he added.

This was a miracle. I had survived death on the raid, and now I had narrowly escaped death again. This man was a killer. His eyes were always bloodshot, and killing seemed like a game to him.

Surely there was a reason I had escaped death. Maybe I might help change the ten-year-old war that has made people think peace in northern Uganda is only a dream. War has made so much pain in the hearts of people. They crave peace. Their tears roll down their faces every day. Hands are lifted high for help, but it makes no difference. Children are dragged into the bush and taught to smash people's heads and cut people's lips, hands and limbs.

Other children live on the streets. They walk with their hands open so that somebody might drop a leftover to quench their hunger. Their restaurants are the dust bins. They do not know how warm a blanket can be because they are constantly in the cold. They have no medical treatment, no school. They are stripped of all human rights and the right to be children. These children don't know what it means to love because they have never been shown love. Their parents were killed when they were so young that they don't know what their faces looked like.

But on the day of my escape I was thinking most about us, those who were dragged like a goat and taken to the rugged, arid land of South Sudan, never to see the faces of their parents.

My thoughts were drifting again; this would not help me. I must think of getting out of here. With a harsh voice, my husband ordered me to go cook for him. "I want food. Go." I had nothing to cook, so I had to go look for leaves. *Sister Rachele maybe is struggling to find us out here*, I thought. I went for wild leaves, climbing trees to get the more tender leaves. I was so tired.

It was during this time that I tried shooting myself three times. Every time I tried to pull the trigger of the gun, God brought someone to grab the gun away from me. It was not yet time for me to die.

12

Creating Killer Children

faith:

> "The children must be able to forgive others and themselves."

Violence such as this is only part of the evil that Joseph Kony is spreading throughout northern Uganda, southern Sudan and other parts of east Africa. In addition to the actions themselves, the fact that Kony uses the young children he has abducted and trained to be killers is an evil beyond comprehension.

Kony's movement did not long remain an army of adult soldiers like Alice Auma's Holy Spirit Mobile Force. The Acholi quickly discovered that they wanted no part in Kony's war. He had coerced, forced and persuaded as many former UPDA soldiers to join him as he could, and that source of cannon fodder was depleted. So he took the children of the very Acholi he had claimed to be fighting for. As many as 90 percent of the LRA's soldiers are abducted children and as many as fifty thousand children have been taken for this purpose by Kony since 1986. More than one hundred thousand other people, mostly civilians, have been killed by the LRA. Almost the entire population of Acholi land has been confined to internally displaced persons (IDP) camps.

In an article in *Christianity Today*, journalist J. Carter Johnson says that the only reason for the Lord's Resistance Army's continued existence "is to perpetuate the power of its leader."[1] This conclusion is confirmed by the International Crisis Group in their report on northern Uganda. They say, "The LRA is not motivated by any identifiable political agenda, and its military strategy and tactics reflect this. Although it does occasionally evoke Acholi nationalism and emancipation, these are irreconcilable with its violence against the Acholi."[2]

An idea of the level of violence suffered by the Acholi at the hands of the LRA comes from the reports of the attacks on Acholi citizens, the abduction of children and the cruel program of turning those children into ruthless killing machines. "Perhaps the greatest atrocity is teaching these children that they spread this carnage by the power of the Holy Spirit to purify the 'unrepentant,' twisting Christianity into a religion of horror to their victims," says Johnson.[3]

The LRA attacks villages, refugee camps, schools, seminaries, hospitals and other undefended facilities. Amnesty International reports that schools are a favorite target of the LRA. In June 2003, they attacked Lacor Seminary and abducted forty seminarians.[4] Grace Akallo's abduction was at St. Mary's School in Aboke. Amnesty International reports that between 1993 and July 1996, seventy teachers were killed by the LRA in Kitgum District. In just two months of 1996, eleven teachers and more than one hundred children were killed in Gulu District. In addition, two hundred fifty primary school children were abducted, and fifty-nine primary schools were burned.[5]

When the LRA attacks, the parents and other adults often are killed immediately. Frequently they are hacked to pieces with pangas, and their homes are burned. As terrible as these incidents are, it is better to die at the hands of a stranger than to live long enough as a prisoner to see your child being forced at gunpoint to murder you. This is a tactic Kony uses to dehumanize children.

A *Christian Research Journal* report on northern Uganda says that the LRA "operates as a fear-based authoritarian military cult."[6] The child's fear, which begins with abduction, doesn't end until the child's conscience has been totally deadened through witnessing and participating in acts of torture, mutilation and murder.

After the abduction, the children are tied up and marched through the bush for days. Their destination is usually the LRA's base camp in Sudan. They are forced to carry heavy supplies and the booty gained in the rebels' attack. The children march from morning until night in their bare feet, without food or water. While the commanders have drinking water, the children are forced to drink urine or water from muddy ditches. A child who becomes ill or cannot keep up is killed. A child who tries to escape or is caught crying is killed. The other children must carry out the execution.

Each succeeding moment in the children's lives is used to indoctrinate, transforming them into Kony's band of killers. When they are forced to carry out a killing, they do not shoot the victim. Death is as painful as possible. Usually the child is hacked to death with a machete or beaten with clubs or sticks. Children who refuse to participate in the killing may also be beaten or killed.[7]

LRA commanders often force children to kill their own siblings, just to ensure that the children's loyalty will be to the movement, not to family. The leaders require every abducted child to kill another child within a week of being captured. This helps to create alienation against society in the mind of the child. A child who has killed someone is told by the commander that he or she must now stay with the LRA forever in order to survive.[8]

Kill or be killed is only one of the lessons that these children are forced to learn. Many of the boys are severely traumatized when forced to rape women that they capture in ambushes. And the children are regularly beaten in order to harden them for battle, some so savagely that they are disfigured for life, says J. Carter Johnson.[9] A cycle of fear and guilt keeps the children captive until it is no longer needed. Either the transformation to killer is complete, or the child is dead.

There is a dilemma about what is to become of children who are rescued or who escape from the LRA. Northern Uganda lacks the proper conditions to bring healing and normality, particularly when those at home are still vulnerable to the LRA. Humanitarian organizations such as World Vision attempt to provide counseling to returnees, but no group has the resources to provide adequate therapy. Without proper trauma counseling and spiritual and emotional healing, these children are in danger of further tragedy.[10]

Children who have escaped or been rescued from the LRA, as well as adults who have had the chance to desert, are promised amnesty by the Ugandan government. The rebels have told the children that if they return to society they will be executed for

Betty Bigombe (left), the chief mediator between the LRA and the government of Uganda, attends GuluWalk in Washington, D.C., with Michael Poffenberger. Bigombe, a former government minister, has led several initiatives to contact Joseph Kony and begin peace negotiations and has worked together with the Acholi religious leaders to assure amnesty for LRA defectors. (Photo by Faith McDonnell)

their crimes, but this is just one more of Kony's lies. Thanks to an international campaign of pressure by the Acholi Religious Leaders Peace Initiative, the Ugandan government passed the Amnesty Act in 2000, giving amnesty to any LRA rebel who surrenders and denounces the rebellion.

Rehabilitation and Reintegration Treatment

A provision of the Amnesty Act is that those who return are known as "reporters." When they return, abductees must report to the Ugandan army (UPDF) or one of the local counselors (LC). They will then spend a number of days being debriefed by the UPDF. After that, most of the escapees and defectors are brought to a counseling center that attempts to provide a "rehabilitation and reintegration psychosocial program."[11]

Both Kitgum and Gulu have centers to care for former fighters and captives. One of the centers in Gulu, Children of War Rehabilitation Center, is run by the Christian relief and development organization World Vision. The World Vision center, which has worked with 11,500 children in its eleven years of existence, has become so well known that LRA commanders try to stop their abductees from going there. The commanders say that if they run away from the rebels and go to the center they will be killed by the people who work at the center with a lethal injection or poison in their food.[12]

Although the World Vision center and the other centers are supported by a number of international nongovernmental organizations and donors, they work closely with the local Acholi community. The Acholi want to help their children find peace and sanity again. Psychosocial counseling, traditional Acholi practices of forgiveness and reconciliation and the message of forgiveness offered by Christ come together in the work of rehabilitation and reintegration.

Children receive medical care and nutritious food at the centers. After months or years of abuse and near-starvation in the bush, rehabilitation has to start with physical needs. The children then receive psychological counseling and vocational training. In the World Vision center, they are also shown the love of Christ in a way that displaces the false and perverted form of religion perpetrated by the Lord's Resistance Army. "Workers model Christian love and forgiveness in everything they do with the children, slowly showing them how to forgive the unforgivable in others and themselves," says journalist J. Carter Johnson.[13]

The Christian message does not provide any shortcuts in the slow process of psychological counseling. Returnees suffer from post-traumatic stress disorder (PTSD), symptoms of which include nightmares, anxiety, flashbacks and aggressive and even violent behavior. Counselors are trained in PTSD therapy. A World Vision staff specialist trains counselors specifically in how children will react after experiencing the kind of atrocities committed by the LRA.[14]

At the Children of War Center, returnees unable to express their feelings or to actually tell what has happened to them are encouraged to draw pictures. Examples of these drawings, depicting life before, during and after abduction, are shown in World Vision's northern Uganda report, *Pawns of Politics: Children, Conflict, and Peace in Northern Uganda.*[15] A particularly compelling view of life as an abductee is at the website of the International Rescue Committee.[16] The use of such art therapy eventually enables the children to begin talking about what happened to them.

Because the need is so great, the time in posttrauma counseling allotted for each returnee ranges from one to three months. Counselors at all the centers lament that children need more time to prepare to rejoin society, but some time in a center is better than no time at all.

Posttreatment follow-up studies show that children who have received counseling in a center have much better mental and emotional health and social readjustment than children who go home without treatment after returning from abduction. Johnson relates that some children at the Children of War Center had gone directly home, but they could not adjust to normal life, even years later. Finally their families sent them to the center "when their symptoms ma[d]e life an impossible, daily nightmare."[17] The director of the World Vision center, Michael Oruni, told of one boy who was brought to the center by his family after he had broken bones in both of his hands by punching the walls of his house.

Children who did go to the center before returning home generally reported that the counseling helped them readjust to the community. One youth said:

> World Vision cared for me and gave me everything I needed. The most positive thing was it helped me [learn] how to live in the community. I don't incite other people. I am obedient to my parents, I don't mix with other bad boys. I live a good life. The counseling was good, they taught us about child rights, and that people should love one another.[18]

Justice and Forgiveness

At the Children of War Center, good counseling is complemented by the good news of God's forgiveness. The most difficult obstacle to overcome on the journey to recovery and healing has to do with forgiveness. The children must be able to forgive others and themselves. Concepts of forgiveness and reconciliation are deeply rooted in Acholi culture, and groups like the Acholi Religious Leaders Peace Initiative and the Concerned Parents' Association stress this need.

It is, however, easier to talk about forgiveness than to live it out in an individual life. Johnson says that this kind of forgiveness can take place only when children are able to admit what they have done, accept that they are forgiven for it and forgive others who wronged them.[19]

God will bring complete justice someday for all that the victims of the LRA have suffered. But for now, how do justice and forgiveness work together? This is the dilemma of a potential peace agreement between Kony and the Ugandan government.

True forgiveness is not denying that no wrong was ever com-

Only love, acceptance and forgiveness can bring the healing that former abductee child mothers such as these need. (Photos by Sarita Hartz)

mitted. It is not saying, "It's all right. It doesn't matter." True forgiveness is much sharper and cleaner than those denials that are sometimes misrepresented as forgiveness. In true forgiveness there is freedom. Forgiveness says, "These things that happened are all true, but in spite of them, I choose to forgive." This is the kind of freedom the former abductees need.

13

It Was Time to Live

grace:

"I will surely work to stop these red-eyed men."

One evening after coming back from a raid, I needed to cry before God. I was tired of seeing seven-year-old children forced to leave their parents to be in the cold morning or the rain. They are trained to hold a gun, trained to shoot without mercy.

One could tell who had been in the army for years. This was true of the commanders especially but also of some of the children who had been abducted and become part of the LRA for some time. Their lives were filled with nothing but anger and hate. Human beings no longer had any value in their eyes. So their eyes changed. Constant anger made their eyes red and bloodshot.

The soldiers with red and bloodshot eyes are no longer children but killers. They look at even their parents as enemies. *What kind of future will northern Uganda have if these people are again part of our people?* I wondered.

I did not learn to be angry. I lived for a long time only in hopelessness. I assumed I would die of starvation or thirst. Or I would be beaten to death with sticks and pangas, or machetes. This is why I was disappointed when the others thought I had died of thirst and buried me. It was hard to come back from the dead, only to suffer longer and know that someday I would die for real.

I saw the body of Paul and was angry that he could be at peace while I had to struggle on. I did not know Paul, but I despaired when he died, because I did not die. I did not understand why.

There were others who felt as I did. They usually found a way to kill themselves. Suicides were common. Once in the camp I turned a gun on myself and would have quickly shot myself, but someone was nearby and snatched the gun out of my grasp. Once we were on a raid, and I did not want to go on, so I again tried to kill myself with my gun. And once again someone was standing nearby and took the gun away before I could.

This was a remarkable thing. It was not normal for someone to care about a soldier who killed herself. We didn't help one another at all. We couldn't or we would be beaten. The Aboke girls tried to stay together and encourage one another when they could. But we couldn't help others. It wasn't natural that someone would stop me from killing myself. And this happened not once, but twice.

The only answer is that God saved my life, and I began turning to Him in my heart for help. He gave me hope that one day I might be able to escape. Or else I would find peace in death.

"God, if You let me go back, I will surely work to stop these red-eyed men from coughing under the bush like a monkey looking for bananas and mangoes," I prayed. "I will fight for the children who become victims in this war. They cannot speak. They are waiting for someone to rescue them from pain. They wait until their skin dries up and their sockets swallow their eyes. Their home is somebody's porch at night and by day their table is in the trash bin."

I went to my trench to sleep. I tied the strap of my gun around me and lay down.

I began praying. I cried to Him and worshiped in all the ways I could think of, only under my breath for fear of being heard. I said, "Please, Jesus, let me have a glimpse of my parents. Then I will come to You in peace." In my prayers, tears rolled down my cheeks. By myself when I prayed was the only time I cried. But the biggest cry was deep down in my heart.

The night when I prayed these things I had a dream that I was crossing a river with other children, but I was the only one who managed to cross to the other side. God was giving me a sign, a sign to go home. But how? He knew, and He just renewed my faith.

In the morning after prayers and the dream, I met my friend Judith on the way to get water for my husband. I told her I was going home. I also told her not to ask me how because I didn't know. I encouraged her to pray and wait for the right time that God had set for us. Several times God had rescued me over the last seven months of toil and danger.

It was time to live.

14

Experiences That Leave Scars

faith:

> "Coming out of the bush is just the
> first step in a long road to healing and
> restoration."

Imagine being abducted in the middle of the night.
Imagine a friend or a sister or brother forced to march bare-foot through a wilderness of rocks and thick trees for days at a time with no food or water.

Imagine that it is your daughter or son who must make a decision between killing another child, perhaps one of their own playmates, or being killed. Many parents in northern Uganda do not even know whether their children are alive or dead. They are simply lost to the parents who love them, to their family and friends. They may be buried alive in a mass grave of terror and captivity.

Human Rights Watch gathered testimonies from formerly abducted children that give graphic insight into what the children of northern Uganda have endured at the hands of Joseph Kony and the LRA. Following are a few examples from their report, "The Scars of Death."[1]

Susan, sixteen years old

One boy tried to escape, but he was caught. They made him eat a mouthful of red pepper, and five people were beating him. His hands were tied, and then they made us, the other new captives, kill him with a stick. I felt sick. I knew this boy from before. We were from the same village. I refused to kill him, and they told me they would shoot me. They pointed a gun at me, so I had to do it. The boy was asking me, "Why are you doing this?" I said I had no choice. After we killed him, they made us smear his blood on our arms. I felt dizzy. There was another dead body nearby, and I could smell the body. I felt so sick. They said we had to do this so we would not fear death and so we would not try to escape.

Timothy, fourteen years old

I was good at shooting. I went for several battles in Sudan. The soldiers on the other side would be squatting, but we would stand in a straight line. The commanders were behind us. They would tell us to run straight into gunfire. The commanders would stay behind and would beat those of us who would not run forward. You would just run forward shooting your gun. I don't know if I actually killed any people. . . . In Sudan we were fighting the

Dinkas and other Sudanese civilians. I don't know why we were fighting them. We were just ordered to fight.

Charles, fifteen years old

There had already been rumors that rebels were around, and we were very fearful. My grandmother was hiding in the bush. It was morning and I was practicing my music when I heard a shot. I started running into the bush, but there was a rebel hiding behind a tree. I thought he would shoot me. He said, "Stop, my friend, don't try to run away!" Then he beat me with the handle of the gun on my back. He ordered me to direct him and told me that afterward I would be released. But afterward it was quite different. That afternoon we met with a very huge group of rebels, together with so many new captives. We marched and marched. In the bush we came across three young boys who had escaped from the rebels earlier, and they removed the boys' shirts and tied ropes around their throats, so that when they killed them they would make no noise. Then they forced them down and started clubbing their heads, and other rebels came with bayonets and stabbed them. It was not a good sight.

William, ten years old

It was at 7 P.M. We were in the house, and two of us were abducted. It was me and my older brother. My mother was crying, and they beat her. She was weak, and I do not know if she is all right at all. They beat us, then they made me carry some radios and carry the commander's gun. It was heavy, and at first I was afraid it would shoot off in my arms, but it was not filled with ammunition. We joined a big group and we walked very far, and my feet were very swollen. If you said that you were hurting, they would say, "Shall we give this young boy a rest?" But by a "rest" they meant they would kill you, so if you did not wish to die you had to say you did not need a rest. Many children tried to escape and were killed. They made us help. I was afraid and I missed my mother. But my brother was very strong-hearted and he told me we must have courage; we will not die. So I kept going.

Christine, seventeen years old

It was around 2 or 3 o'clock in the night. I woke to the sound of windows breaking and torches flashing. I don't know how many rebels there were. Some of us were beaten. I was shaking. . . . We walked the whole night, through the bush and on small paths. While we were walking, they would kick us or slap us or hit us with gun butts and sometimes with sticks. Whenever they killed anyone, they called us to watch. I saw eleven people killed this way. One of them was a boy who had escaped. They found him in his home and called him outside. They made him lie down on the ground, and they pierced him with a bayonet. They chopped him with the bayonet until he was dead. Seeing this, at times I felt like I was a dead person—not feeling anything. And then sometimes I would feel like it was happening to me, and I would feel the pain.

These testimonies are typical of thousands of stories of what has been done to northern Uganda's children and what they have been forced to do. Children who had been playing soccer with their schoolmates, going to church with their families and giggling with their best friends may be forced to kill someone they know and love.

Other stories reveal more of the appalling demands of Kony and his commanders. In one case, a girl told of having to attempt to bite to death another child who tried to escape. When, after being bitten by a number of other children, she was still not dead, they had to finish killing her with a stick.[2] In another, a boy of twelve had to participate in the killing of an eleven-year-old boy who had complained that he was tired while carrying a heavy load of stolen food. They were forced to chop the boy, foot by foot and hand by hand. Then they were told to slice off his eyelids with razor blades. While the boy was still conscious, they hung him up on a tree and were told to box his head until he was dead.[3]

While boys abducted by the LRA are used as porters and soldiers, girls have the added horror of being "given as wives" to commanders. The LRA is one of the worst sex traffickers in a world where sex trafficking is a huge enterprise. In the 2006 Trafficking in Persons Report issued by the United States Department of State's Office of Trafficking in Persons, the country narrative for Uganda says:

> The terrorist rebel organization Lord's Resistance Army (LRA) abducts children and adults in northern Uganda and southern Sudan to serve as cooks, porters, agricultural workers, and combatants; girls are subjected to sex slavery and forced marriage. Some abducted children and adults remain within Uganda, while others are taken to southern Sudan or eastern Democratic Republic of the Congo.[4]

Heike Behrend observes, "In a way, practices of the nineteenth century slave trade are reinforced by the LRA."[5]

Amnesty International adds that one of the main reasons for which the LRA takes girls is to use them for forced "marriage" to the senior LRA soldiers and commanders. Good soldiers and top leaders are rewarded with "wives." Amnesty International says that the number of "wives" a rebel has is a source of prestige and proof of his status. "The testimony of children describes a strictly hierarchical structure within the LRA founded on a macabre re-ordering of experience familiar to children," says the Amnesty report. "The bedrock of internal organization is what the children describe as the 'family.' This relies, in the end, on the abduction of girls for forced marriage—without forced marriage the 'families' would not exist."[6]

A group of child mothers at Unyama IDP camp in Gulu. These girls range in age from 17 to 24 and spent one to two years in the bush as LRA soldiers. All had either one or two children. (Photo by Sarita Hartz)

The description of the family adds that the girls were forced to carry out all the duties expected of a wife in rural Acholi society. They cook, clean, fetch water and gather food. This might be a tolerable bit of normality in an otherwise intolerable existence, except that the girls are under constant anxiety that they might break one of the LRA's rules. Cooking, for instance, is to be carried out quickly, and the smoke from the cooking fire must not be allowed to be seen. Allowing smoke to be seen carries a death sentence.

Ownership of the girls by the male leaders of the LRA includes the power to give them to another "husband" if the one they belong to is killed in battle or tires of them. Journalist J. Carter Johnson adds that while attractive girls are used as sexual slaves and regularly raped in LRA "marriages," plainer girls are, at times, used for what can only be called "murder practice."[7]

The following testimonies are from Human Rights Watch interviews with girls who had been freed or escaped from the LRA.[8]

Theresa, eighteen years old

I was made to be wife to three men. Three rebels were fighting over me, and each one wanted me to be his wife. One of them wanted to kill me. He took me as his wife, and I did not want to be his wife. He said if I refused he would kill me, and if I ran away he would kill me. He was sent away to fight, and then I was made to be wife to a second man. Then he also was sent away to fight, and I was given to a third man. The third man was a big leader, and when he went away to fight he wanted me to go with him.

Susan, sixteen years old

One week after I was abducted, I was given to a man called Abonga. He was thirty years old. Two girls were given to him. He

133

was trying to be nice to me, to make me feel happy and not want to run away, but all I wanted to do was go home. I was taken away from him when I got to Sudan because I had syphilis. They said they wanted to give me treatment, but I refused—I did not trust them and thought that they might try to hurt me, and I felt fine anyway. Because I had syphilis, I was not given to another man in Sudan. Instead I was kept separately and guarded because they thought I would give the sickness to others. No one was allowed to have free relationships there. If they caught a boy and a girl together they would shoot you in public. The only relationships they allowed were the ones that they forced on you.

Catherine, seventeen years old

They gave us all as wives. I think four of the girls abducted from the St. Mary's School at Aboke were given to Kony as wives; they stayed with Kony's other girls. They gave me as a wife, but I refused the man. The soldier I was given to already had a girl who was five months pregnant. He ordered other boys to beat me on my back with a panga. He hated me. I got eight strokes with the panga on my back. It hurt so much, I thought I would die. After that we never spoke. I just stayed with the other girls.

Evidence collected through testimonies such as these, as well as medical sources, suggests that sexual slavery is imposed on all abducted girls, except possibly girls below thirteen years of age and those who manage to escape within a week of being captured. As a result, those who escape later often are infected with venereal diseases, including HIV/AIDS.

The stigma of rape in Acholi society makes it very difficult for girls to talk about what has been done to them. Amnesty reported that children who were interviewed found it easier to admit to having killed than to having raped or having been raped. A counselor told Amnesty International that all the girls deny being raped at first, but eventually they will admit it.[9]

For a child, denying the trauma inflicted upon him or her—whether the trauma of being turned into a killer or of sexual abuse—is a kind of self-protection. While in captivity, a boy or girl may pay for tears or any other sign of weakness with death. The

Acholi mothers and their children. Many former child soldiers are now child mothers. Freed from captivity by the LRA, these young women have to overcome trauma, abuse, stigmatization and rejection to make a new life for themselves and their children. (Photos by Sarita Hartz)

mind and spirit need to be shielded from the reality that is taking place. In a desperate attempt at survival, a child withdraws into himself or herself.

135

That self-protection eventually can be an obstacle that must be surmounted in order for healing to take place. Often, when children are rescued, their minds and spirits fear to leave that interior place to which they have been fleeing when in bondage. Coming out of the bush is just the first step in a long road to healing and restoration. The life of Grace Akallo shows that such a journey is possible, but it is not an easy road. Many children who are rescued do not finish the journey. They become lifelong casualties to the violence of the LRA.

15

Escape from the Kony Nightmare

grace:
"God was carrying me on His back when
I thought I was walking by myself."

The rebel leader Joseph Kony called for an assembly by the
holy tree. It was not the first time he had called people under
this tree. It was the same as church on Sunday and mosque on
Friday. It was also the place for public address. We were required
to remove our gun magazines and even our sandals—for those
who had sandals—and leave them far away from the holy tree.

This tree was where Kony told people what his spirits had said
to him. It was where he brought new children and told them
he was the representative of God, and God wanted Uganda to
be ruled by the Ten Commandments. He would instruct his

commander to smear the children with nut butter and use an unbroken egg's shell to paint them with ash mixed with water. This was to initiate them into the system and give them protection. It was called camouflage. This ritual, plus the beating that went with it, put a deep fear into the hearts of the children. The children would bear the buried fear until they were free and the last of their shadows had disappeared.

"There are seven hundred rebels coming to attack us," Kony announced as he walked gracefully, like an enthroned king, in his combatant uniform. "They are weak, and we will only send one hundred soldiers to drive them off," he added.

My mind started singing. I prayed that this would be my chance for the freedom that I knew was coming. I don't know where I got the idea, but it gave me hope. I started praying for God to open the way for me.

Kony said, "We should be on standby." That meant that we must be prepared to fight. More bullets were given, and he instructed the soldiers. After his address he dismissed us to go prepare. He told his commanders to distribute guns to those who didn't have one and more bullets to everyone. My gun stuck on my side like a book and pen ready for exams when I left the distribution site.

"Come here," Raska Lokuya called after me. "You girls are the ones bringing this problem here," he said as he approached me. "You should be killed, and we will see why you are more important than the others. Why are they after you and not the other children? Does it mean that the other children are not important? I am going to kill you myself if you dare to escape." His threat scared me, but it did not stop my determination to get to freedom. He took my gun from me but gave it back later because everyone was expected to fight.

Why were the Aboke girls singled out? It was because of Sister Rachele, who publicized our abduction. We were talked about on the radio all the time. Naturally the commanders didn't understand why people around the world cared for this one group of girls. Some of them perhaps understood that the world looked at us and saw all the rest of the abducted children as well. People could not understand the thousands of missing children. It was too much to comprehend. But they could identify with thirty schoolgirls. This is why the commanders hated us. We showed the world what they were doing.

One hundred children were sent to meet these people that Kony called rebels. None of the children came back. They were all killed. A group of Arab soldiers who had gone with them came back, running for their lives. They raced past our camp, yelling in Arabic. To me the words sounded like prayers. They actually were saying that things were not good behind them, and they were running to Juba, a small, nearby town in Sudan.

Kony was a proud man, and he was trying to make his name great with the Sudan government. He was supposed to fight the SPLA in exchange for the guns that the government of Sudan gave him. So he sent some more children. Again, few children managed to come back. All the others perished. Now Kony realized that he was about to be caught. He fled to Juba in the car that had been given to him by the government of Sudan.

He left the children to die.

It looked like the end had come. Everybody was running, confused. There was nowhere to hide because the bullets were flying everywhere and hitting anybody who happened to be in the way. Huts were burning in the camp. With the baggage on their heads and cooking pans and guns strapped on their sides, some tried to march away. Most of them fell down like dry leaves and were trampled by the ones who were running to save their lives. Many were left lying in a pool of blood with no one to cover them. I saw mothers dying. The children strapped to their backs were wondering when their mother was going to get up. Some children tried to suckle a dead mother.

Just watching this scene made me want to give up. I had been sent to fight and had seen many people die—children, mothers and all. Nothing had prepared me for this. I waited for my time. I looked around to take in every bit of my surroundings before I died. I did not run like the others. I had lost the hope that had kept me going, the hope of going home and seeing my mother again.

As fear crept into my heart, a strange voice tortured me: *How can you come out of this? Who are you? Do you think you are different from the other people?* It was the dark spirit that was speaking, giving me deep fears that not even my mother could save me from. It reminded me of the little girl we had been forced to kill one week after our abduction. It was the inside fight that hurt me more than the outside fight; the inside fight made me feel guilty.

I groaned in my heart, *God, if You love me, please help me. Jesus, if You love me, take me home.* The bullets were flying over my head, but none hit me. Yet the fight within hit me hard.

When God says yes, no one can say no. It was my day of freedom. It was the day He wanted me to know that He was with me and I was not going to die. My prayers had reached Him and He had heard me. A quiet voice whispered to me in clear words, commanding yet not forceful: *Get up and move away from here.* It was hard differentiating this quiet voice from the voice that had scared me. But it was comforting.

I obeyed the gentle voice, picked up my gun, tied my cooking pans on my back, picked up the pack given to me by Agnes, one of my husband's wives, and walked across the camp.

A stray bullet hit a cooking pan strapped on my back. I thought I was dead. I fell down and lay still like a dead body. It seemed my soul had jumped away a little bit. I could still hear the gunshots, but I thought I was dead. I was in shock.

The gentle voice whispered to me again and told me to get up. Slowly I got up and looked at my back. There was no blood flowing from my back. It was the third time I had survived when I thought I was dead. I picked up only the gun and walked on. I never looked back at the ruins or the dead bodies I left behind. I did not know where I was going. I was not escaping, but God was leading me home. I did not know it at the time, but God was carrying me on His back when I thought I was walking by myself.

16

Who Is Protecting Us?

faith:

"Most children have never known life outside the packed squalor of the camps."

Two decades have gone by in Joseph Kony's war against the Acholi. Hundreds of thousands have been left dead or mutilated. Children have been abducted. Who is protecting the people of northern Uganda? As peace talks continue endlessly, most of the Acholi people have distant memories of life in their own villages, tending their own livestock and crops. Most children have never known life outside the packed squalor of the camps. They have never experienced the stable life that Grace Akallo remembers when she was small, of traditions passed down from grandparents by an evening fire.

The government promised those moved to refugee camps that they would be safe from rebel raids, killing and abductions by living in concentrated areas where soldiers could be nearby to help. That isn't the way it has turned out. Rebels kill and kidnap with the same impunity at the camps as when people lived scattered across northern Uganda. Many cynically believe that mass relocation in internally displaced persons (IDP) camps is a political solution to suppress the Acholi. It feels to the Acholi as if two wars are being waged against them. They are trapped between the brutality of the Lord's Resistance Army and the prejudice and failed solutions imposed by the government.

Rather than having sanctuary, children feel no safety at all in their homes at the IDP camps. Any night they could be dragged away into the bush. Without traditional protection from family, clan chiefs and government, the children have been forced to take steps to protect themselves as best they can. Many thousands of children have become "night commuters."

Olara A. Otunnu, the former UN Under-Secretary-General and Special Representative for Children and Armed Conflict, voices the fears and beliefs of many that the Ugandan government is cynically using the LRA's activities "to divert attention from what is happening in the government's concentration camps."[1] Otunnu believes that the government is continuing the cycle of violence and retaliation seen over the history of Uganda by forcing the Acholi into IDP camps.

"The Acholi people are renowned for their deep-rooted and rich culture, values system, and family structure," says Otunnu. And "all these have been destroyed under the living conditions prevailing over the last ten years in the camps." He concludes that "this loss is colossal and virtually irreparable; it signals the death of a people and their civilization."[2]

A similar concern was voiced to Baroness Caroline Cox on her fact-finding visit to northern Uganda in February 2006.[3] "There have been 20 years of suffering, perceived by the population as 'slow genocide'—and they feel that no one beyond the region knows or cares," Lady Cox said in her report. "They point out that, in the 1990s, when many cattle died in a part of Uganda where the President comes from, it was declared a 'Disaster Area.' 'When animals were dying, it was declared a Disaster Area; here, people are dying in huge numbers and it is not yet declared a Disaster Area.'"[4]

More than 1.7 million Acholi, almost the entire population of the region, are displaced. Whether their deplorable conditions are deliberately orchestrated by the government or are due to indifference, the result is the same to the Acholi. No one protects them from slowly but gradually dying in the IDP camps, and no

A northern Ugandan IDP camp: a breeding ground for disease and despair. (Photo by Sarita Hartz)

one protects them sufficiently from ongoing attacks by the LRA, even within the camps.

While some have gone to the camps voluntarily to escape the LRA, others have been "herded like animals into concentration camps."[5] There are about two hundred camps in the region, all of which offer horrendous, cramped living conditions.

Dying in the Camps

Mortality rates in these areas are high, exceeding the "emergency threshold," according to "Health and Mortality Survey among Internally Displaced Persons in Gulu, Kitgum, and Pader Districts, Northern Uganda."[6] The survey was conducted by the World Health Organization, UNICEF, the World Food Program, the United Nations Population Fund and the International Rescue Committee. Almost one thousand people die each week in the camps. In fact, the mortality rates in northern Uganda are double those for displaced person camps for the Darfurians of western Sudan, where Islamist-backed tribes have waged genocidal warfare against tribes with tacit government support. As bad as the situation is in Darfur, at least there are two hundred aid agencies that work there, while only sixty are active in northern Uganda.

In her testimony to the House International Relations Committee, U.S. House of Representatives, Michelle Brown, the senior advocate and UN representative for Refugees International, stated, "The Government of Uganda has the primary responsibility to assist and protect internally displaced persons in northern Uganda, and it has clearly failed in fulfilling its responsibility." Brown continued that when she had visited northern Uganda, she had seen "no indication that the government has taken significant concrete steps to improve living conditions in camps."[7]

In the IDP camps there is no access to adequate health care. Neither do people have sufficient food and water, sanitation, education, protection or employment. Cox comments, "The system of camps could aptly be described as a vast 'hot Gulag Archipelago.'"[8]

The camps are terribly overcrowded, a result of an assumption that if there is safety in numbers, people should have their huts close to one another. Usually six or eight people share a small, round grass-thatched hut that is roughly six and one-half feet in diameter. Huts built so close together easily catch and spread fire. Huts burn in cooking fires and other accidents regularly at such locations as Pabbo Camp, one of the largest IDP camps in East Africa. Sixty thousand people live in Pabbo Camp. At any one time, thousands may be homeless because of hut fires. In early 2003, one fire consumed three thousand huts, leaving ten thousand people homeless. Other fires, designed to kill as well as leave people homeless, have been set by the LRA.

Pawns of Politics, World Vision's study of northern Uganda, reports that in the IDP camps, the most likely diseases that affect the population and the most likely causes of death are "largely preventable and curable, indicating weak health services."[9] People in northern Uganda are twice as likely to experience diarrhea as people in the rest of the country. This is likely due to the fact that as many as four thousand people may share a latrine. Infant mortality rose from 99 to 106 deaths per 1,000 births between 1995 and 2000.

Integrated Regional Information Networks (IRIN), a news organization attached to the United Nations that updates humanitarian organizations on African and Asian events, interviewed James, a camp leader in Kitgum District. He was asked about health issues in his camp and asked that any available

A small section of one of northern Uganda's overcrowded and dirty IDP camps. In the foreground is one of the few "toilet" facilities—a hole in the ground. Disease runs rampant due to the lack of proper sanitation. (Photo by Sarita Hartz)

NGO be sent to help set up clinics. "It could help our children. There is a lot of malaria and coughing. There is also a lot of malnutrition due to poor diet. There are very many people with HIV/AIDS-related illnesses," he said.[10] In fact, malnutrition rates for children in the IDP camps range from 7 percent to 21 percent. Although Uganda as a nation has aggressively worked to reduce the rate of HIV/AIDS infection, the rate of HIV/AIDS in northern Uganda is 11.9 percent, almost double the national average of 6.2 percent.[11]

None of the camps have adequate medical facilities. In Kitgum Matidi IDP camp, which had 31,972 residents in late 2004, there was only one health center, staffed by one nurse, two nursing aides and some community volunteers. The situation is similar in the other camps.[12]

In testimony before the United States House of Representatives International Relations Committee, Michelle Brown said that international standards dictate that IDP camp residents need a minimum of fifteen liters of water a day for drinking, cooking and personal hygiene. Most of northern Uganda's displaced persons have only half that amount.[13] The available water comes from bore holes, wells that have been bored or drilled to reach an underground source of fresh water. People in the camps sometimes wait as long as twelve hours to fill their large jerrican water containers. As many as fifteen thousand people share a water source.[14]

Grinding the Faces of the Poor

"'What do you mean by crushing my people and grinding the faces of the poor?' declares the Lord, the LORD Almighty" (Isaiah 3:15).

It is a bitter irony for the people of northern Uganda to be dependent upon anyone for food. Elijah, a seventy-year-old man living at an IDP camp near Gulu, said to IRIN news:

We hardly have anything to eat. Before this war, Acholi people were not used to depending on relief food. We did a lot of things on our own. Now we can't do the same things we did to survive. Even the food WFP shares out will go to the rebels if you don't hide some of it. They always tell us that it is because of them that we receive humanitarian food. So they have to take the food away, because it does not belong to us. When they don't find food, they get very angry.[15]

Confined to the camps, the Acholi have had to leave their farmlands lying in waste. Cultivated land has reverted to bush. "Insecurity threatens food security, turning areas that were once known as the 'breadbasket' of Uganda into a no-man's land and

148

rendering the population almost wholly dependent on international food aid," says World Vision.[16] Pedro Amolat, head of the World Food Program office in Gulu, reports that only 4 percent of 10,031 square miles arable land in Gulu District is being farmed. The other 96 percent is going to waste because of the war. The land taken out of production would cover an area about the size of Rwanda—about one-third of Uganda.[17]

Farming that has been able to continue is done with extreme difficulty because of the loss of livestock. Acholi land had been a cattle-based economy before the war. As among their neighbors to the north, the Dinka of southern Sudan, cattle were a source of prestige and wealth for the Acholi. The sale of livestock provided the needed funds for family expenses, from children's education to medical bills and other emergency costs. Now the Acholi farmers barely even have the memory of what it was to be independent. It has been many years since most lived in their own house, took care of their own family and had pride in their land and livestock. Other than food gathered from fruit trees and small gardens they cultivate around the camps, the displaced Acholi are dependent on food aid from relief groups. Delivery of food is precarious because of LRA attacks. It is often delayed or cannot take place at all.

Education for children in the camps is also uncertain at best. Many schools have had to close because of fear of the LRA. Other schools have been destroyed by the rebels. Children are supposed to have free education through the completion of primary school, whether in towns or IDP camps of northern Uganda. Because so many schools have closed, there is not room for all the children in the remaining schools. For example, in late 2004 in Bobi Camp, near Gulu, there was one school with 2,500 pupils. An additional 1,800 children could not attend because of the lack of space. In Kitgum Matidi IDP camp, twenty schools forced to close had been combined into two learning centers.

Secondary education is not free. Acholi who used to be able to pay the school fees for their children no longer have any income and so cannot afford to send their children to school.

This contributes to the prevalent feelings of hopelessness and despair in the camps. The lack of available education seems to condemn future generations of the Acholi to more of the misery they are now enduring.[18]

Activist Kelly Lichoff.
(Photo courtesy of Bol B. Aweng and Simon Dau)

Endless Attacks

Supposedly this forced confinement of most of the 1.8 million Acholi has at least made them safer from attack. They should have easier, swifter access to protection by the Ugandan army, the UPDF. The philosophy is that diffusing military forces over all areas that may be raided by the LRA makes it more difficult for the UPDF to monitor conditions and prevent attacks. In reality, people in the camps are scarcely any safer than they were when they lived in the rural areas. The LRA attack IDP camps just as they attacked rural villages, and the UPDF has not offered adequate protection.

One well-documented example from the 1990s still describes the danger. The LRA attacked Atiak trading center in northern Gulu District before dawn on April 22, 1995. The local defense forces that guarded the center were quickly overcome, leaving the civilian population defenseless. Most accounts say that more than two hundred people were killed in that attack. One of the survivors of the massacre, Catherine Akwero, believes that as many as two hundred fifty were murdered. She was interviewed by *New Vision*, Uganda's leading Internet news source.[19]

Akwero recalls that once the defense forces were killed or had fled, the civilians were forced outside. The rebel commander, Vincent Otti, actually came from Atiak, yet he threatened to set the houses on fire. The people were forced to carry all of the food and other goods that the LRA was stealing from them for about six miles out into the bush. At that point, Akwero says, Otti commanded them to stop and sit down. He then radioed LRA contacts and boasted of his accomplishment: "We have carried out a successful operation in Atiak. We abducted so many people, including students. We are going to show them our work."

Otti then addressed the people he had abducted, Akwero says, telling them, "You are useless people. You say our guns are rusting. We shall test them on you."

At that point Otti divided the people into two groups. He separated out his own relatives and then pulled out Akwero because she was carrying a baby. They were sent off to the side, and the people in the main group, including Akwero's fourteen-year-old son, were told to lie facedown.

"Otti then gave the order for shooting," Akwero continues. "He counted: one, two, three." The rebels "fired randomly at the people lying down." When they noticed that some were still moving, Otti ordered two more rounds. Then Otti went over to the survivors, asking them, "Have you seen what we have done?" Akwero says that he joked that if they had relatives among the dead they should come and pick up their bodies "so that you can smoke them." Akwero says she later discovered that four people survived the shooting with multiple gunshot wounds.

The rebels were not through, even then. Akwero says that they selected some boys from the survivors to help them carry their loot. Later the bodies of those boys were found. They had all been stabbed. Some were still alive but died in the hospital. Among all those who had died, Akwero says, were forty-five students and three teachers from Atiak Technical School.[20]

Now move forward almost a decade to the "protected" camps. On February 21, 2004, 337 people, mostly women and children, were killed when Barlonyo IDP Camp, which was protected only by a small local defense unit, was attacked by the LRA. This was the largest LRA massacre of civilians since the start of the conflict. Many were forced to stay inside their huts when the LRA burned them. Whole families were burned alive together.[21]

Less than two weeks before, they had attacked Abia IDP Camp. LRA rebels came into the camp in broad daylight, disguised as "Amuka boys," members of a new local militia that had just been created to protect the camp. Inside the camp, they began shooting, killing fifty people and seriously injuring seventy. Both of these attacks took place in Lira District.[22]

During 2004, the anxiety for the Acholi increased when the rebels changed their tactics. Instead of attacks by large groups, they began moving in smaller groups. George Canopwonya, chairman of Kitgum Matidi subcounty, told IRIN on October 28, 2004, "They have far less arms, but the smaller groups are more vicious towards civilians." Canopwonya told of the abduction of thirteen women and a man who had ventured outside the camp to look for mangoes.[23]

"Each of them had their hands tied behind and were then cut with pangas on the back of the head. We found one baby crying on the back of its dead mother," he said.[24]

Charley Okot, one of the leaders of Lagoro IDP camp, 38 kilometers west of Kitgum, and Alex Odong, the leader of the Bobo IDP camp just outside the town of Gulu, agreed that the LRA is a serious threat to the displaced persons. At the time of his interview in 2004, Okot reported that rebels had just stolen food from the camp garden and abducted four women. Odong warned that rebels disguised in civilian clothes had been spotted.[25]

Despair

Hopelessly living in all this misery, some have committed suicide. The most common victims are mothers who are unable to provide for their children or to protect them from starvation, disease or violence. For example, in August 2005, thirteen mothers committed suicide in Pabbo IDP Camp.[26]

Father Carlos Rodriguez is a Comboni Missionary priest in northern Uganda. He has played a lead role in the Acholi Religious Leaders Peace Initiative and is a courageous advocate for the Acholi. Fr. Rodriguez reported in November 2004 that there were on average three suicides per week in Pabbo. He explained that this was highly unusual for Acholi, whose tradition condemned suicide, but because of the situation they are in, some people see no other option. "Everything Acholi is dying," mourns Fr. Rodriguez.[27]

Olara Otunnu, in his Sydney Peace Prize lecture reprinted in the Kampala *Monitor*, quoted the thoughts of Ugandan journalist Elias Biryabarema after he visited northern Uganda:

Not a single explanation on earth can justify the sickening human catastrophe going on in Lango and Acholi land: the degradation, desolation and the horrors killing off generation after generation. Frankly, it's not entirely imprecise to describe what I saw as a slow extinction facing the Acholi and Langi peoples. I encountered unique and heart-stopping suffering, shocking cruelty and death stalking a people by the minute, by the hour, by the day; for the last two decades. An entire society is being systematically destroyed—physically, culturally, emotionally, socially, and economically—in full view of the international community.[28]

Making Their Own Protection

Who is protecting the children of northern Uganda? Their parents cannot protect them from the Lord's Resistance Army. As we have seen, often the parents are the first to die in LRA violence. The Ugandan government does not seem adequate to the task of protecting the Acholi. The Ugandan government's solution, to confine the Acholi in IDP camps, has merely increased their misery without increasing their security.

When she testified at the United States House of Representatives hearings, Grace Akallo said, "Because no one was protecting them, the children of northern Uganda were making their own protection."[29]

She was referring to the night commuters, thousands of children and young people who come into the towns each night and sleep wherever they can find more security. They may spend the night in the halls or veranda of the town hospital, the bus depot, a church or elsewhere. Recently, shelters have been provided by church groups and human rights organizations. These young people are making their own protection.

For many years, a few northern Ugandans who lived close enough have sought shelter each evening in towns. The phenomenon of a daily mass exodus of night commuters began in 2003. There had been an upsurge in LRA activity, and twelve thousand children had been abducted in the previous year alone. The intensified attacks were Kony's retaliation for the Ugandan government's Operation Iron Fist in 2002.

Children in the rural areas of Acholi, both in the camps and in the villages, have been the most vulnerable to abduction. Most, like Grace Akallo, have been taken in the night when people are most defenseless. Moving into the town centers each night was one way to have some security against the night attacks. Children walk up to ten kilometers before dark to seek shelter in town. Although most of the fifty thousand who have been commuters to Gulu, Kitgum, Lira, Soroti and Pader are children from toddlers to teens, some young mothers with babies and some other adults have joined the night commute.

Mothers and their babies, such as these in Lira, have become night commuters. (Photo by Sarita Hartz)

17

Crossing the River to Uganda

grace:

"God lifted my feet and put them on the
growing grass in the water."

The bushes were quiet. Only the wind was blowing through the
dry, scorched grass and trees, trying to shake the dead leaves.
I thought Sudan was a grave for every living thing. It was the dry
season, and even trees had no life in them. Nature had deprived
them of water and food, and some were destroyed by fires.

I lived with these trees for three days as I walked under them.
I was looking for something to eat. The dead trees could provide
only a little shade with their dry branches. I would sit under them
as if waiting to be dried like them. I was already dry anyway; little
blood flowed in my veins. *After a few days I will be dried up like
the trees*, I thought. I ate soil and leaves of trees that were still

156

struggling to survive. I was hoping to get help from Mother Nature. That is what kept me alive for three days. But it was clear that I was going to die despite escaping all of the death around me. I thought about Paul again and many others who had been left lying under the scorching sun.

"Who are you?" a voice whispered in front of me. I aimed my AK-47 machine gun in the direction the voice came from. I was ready to defend myself.

"I am Grace," I answered. "I am from the home of teacher Lakati," I added. That is what we called the man I was given to as a wife. He had been sent back to Uganda when the camp was attacked. If he had been in the camp, he would have made things very difficult for me.

"Come on over here. Stop pointing your gun at us," the voice said.

"Okay," I answered, but I was still on my guard. Kony had threatened us before that the Holy Spirit would block our way if we tried to escape. Slowly I walked forward. I saw a group of children. Their eyes were misty, yet no tears fell. *We are all walking corpses*, I thought, *condemned to die in this wilderness.*

"Where are you going?" one boy from the group asked me.

"To Uganda," I answered him. But the answer was like a bitter pill in my mouth.

"Are you trying to escape?" one girl asked with suspicion in her voice.

Escape? The way it was said made me think that these children were not trying to run away. I must be careful.

"No," I lied. "I saw people go to Uganda." Really I had not seen any of us going toward Uganda. Many fled toward Juba, but I hoped to convince these children to go with me.

My lie did not work, and one boy pointed his AK-47 at me. "I am going to shoot you," he bawled at me.

"No, you are not," I said to him with a stronger voice than I had known I was capable of. "I have survived from death three times. I survived being beaten to death, I was buried alive and a bullet hit my cooking pans, yet my body was not touched. Who do you think you are to shoot me?" I added, "Go ahead and shoot me. Then I will rest from this suffering."

"Don't bother, she is going to die before reaching Uganda," another boy said. "This is one of the Aboke girls who brought this on us all. Let us leave her here."

Slowly the group of about fifty children walked away from me, their skin slack on their bones. I let them go. I was thinking that they were right. I was going to die here before someone rescued me. I did not know how many days I could survive in this dry land without food or water. I prayed for God to help me. Prayers had become my food and water. It was like I was a scapegoat. I could easily run and hide when I was threatened beyond my control.

As I was deep in my thoughts, wondering whether I was going to survive, one girl from the group came back as if to make sure I had not disappeared. "Are you sure you want to die here?" she asked as she sat near me.

"No," I replied with confidence. "I am going to Uganda."

"Do you know the way?" she asked.

"No, but God will lead me," I told her.

"It seems you know the way. I am going with you," she said.

I looked at the girl, trying to see if she was tricking me into saying that I was escaping. But the girl's eyes were true to her words. She was ready to go with me, even though I did not know the way. "If you are ready, it is okay with me," I answered her.

We quietly sat there together. The deep fears that threatened our very lives were manifested only in our eyes and the way we breathed. *Do you think you will reach Uganda?* A voice within me began tormenting me again. The voice was so loud in my ears and heart, making me lose hope.

We were both startled by the sound of the dry grass breaking. Another girl had come back. Now she sat quietly, as if waiting for some help from me or even a word. I was so tired that I just looked at her quietly with a sigh. I could have started walking away from that place, but something held me down. It was beyond hunger and thirst.

One by one the girls came back and sat near me without a word, as if the spirits would be awakened if anyone spoke. Nine girls came back to me, all expecting some help. None of us knew where it would come from. We were surrounded by evil spirits; spirits of fear had built a home in each of our hearts. We sat for a while looking from one person to another, waiting for someone to speak.

I broke the silence. "What happened? I thought you were going to Juba."

"We thought you knew the way," one girl whose name was Agnes answered me. "We want to go with you," she added.

Without stopping to think, I said, "Let's go." I got up and we started our trek, with our AK-47s strapped to our backs. We walked in silence, falling often because we were all so weak. None of us had eaten for a long time; our eyes had gone deep into our bones. We were no long human beings but dying animals. After walking for a long time, I sat down without a word to my friends. I thought I was going to pass away. I could not speak. My friends without question obeyed the silent order, and all dropped down, some on their stomachs. We were near death.

After a while, I found some strength and managed to tell my friends to sit up to pray. "Can we pray, please?" I asked. It was the first thing I had said since we started our trekking. The girls looked at me strangely but obeyed silently.

"O God, we have no strength. We are thirsty and hungry," I prayed. "Help us out of this hard land, and we will be living examples of Your love. Please help us. Amen."

The girls echoed, "Amen."

After our prayers, it started drizzling. At least some water was dropping from the sky, cooling down the heat that tortured our dry skin. There was a little hope. I felt like we were going to survive. We started walking again, parting the dry grass from our way and trying to put the stalks back to close our trail in case we were being followed. We reached a tributary of the Blue Nile from Sudan. First we were excited because a miracle had happened: We had water. But my heart sank when I realized that none of us could swim. I felt responsible for these kids; they came back to me, thinking I knew the way and would lead them home.

"What are we going to do?" asked Susan, one of the girls who had been quiet since we started this journey.

"I don't know," I answered her.

"I don't know how to swim, and there is no rope to tie on the other side," she said.

"I know." My brain was working, calculating how we might cross the river. This was not the first river I had had to cross since my abduction. Before it was with a group, and there was always someone who knew how to swim to go tie the rope on the other side of the river. But this day we were by ourselves. Groups had crossed the Aswa and Atebi rivers with the aid of the rope. Even then children drowned. A child would slip off the rope and would be washed away like sand. There was no screaming. They were suffocated by the angry water. The rebels felt no loss. I heard them say, "Others will be captured." This was strange to me. In my village, if someone died the whole village would mourn for that person for about two weeks. With the rebels, nobody cared. Life was like waste in the bathroom.

My friends started murmuring, and Agnes spoke up. "You brought us here to die. How are we going to cross this river?"

The others just nodded in response and answered, "Yes."

"You knew all along that you did not know the way, yet you still brought us," another girl interjected. Again, others nodded in agreement.

"We will strangle you before we die," Susan said.

I was not scared of threats. My mind was past fear, yet I was angry with the girls who thought they had a reason to blame me. Did they think I had planned to bring them here to die? I composed myself with strength.

"I told you I did not know the way to Uganda, but I was trusting God to lead me. You agreed to follow me, but it was not because I said I knew the way. I did not force you to come. You just followed me in silence. Now you have turned against me, just because we can't cross the river. You know what? Let us eat the sand and drink water. Maybe we can begin thinking better."

We all turned to eat the soil and drink water, as if it was going to give some miracle. *This is funny*, I thought as I gobbled the soil down and drank water to push it down into my stomach. *We fear death, yet we are walking skeletons. We are trying to run from death when it is already in us.*

"What are you going to do now?" Agnes asked after drinking water to wash down the soil she had eaten.

"I don't know," I murmured, whether to her or to myself. But she heard me.

"Well, if you don't know, we are going to kill you because you are the one who brought us here," Agnes said as she moved closer.

"No, you are not going to strangle me. I am just going to jump into this water and drown," I told her. I moved backward to the river and slipped in. I thought I would drown, but with gentle hands my God lifted my feet and put them on the growing grass in the water. I slowly crossed the river. It was a miracle, but there was no time to think about that. My friends with great surprise followed my way. One by one they crossed the river.

18

Acts of Defiance

A feeling of inevitability has crushed many children of the war years. It is easy for a child to assume that one day soon he or she will be taken by the rebels. When these children are asked if they have been abducted, many of them answer, "Not yet." It is beyond their hopes that they will live through childhood without someday being awakened by the rebels. So the night commuter children, for all of their struggles, are one of the few positive signposts for the future. These children are defying the assumption of hopelessness as they huddle at night in protected shelters. Making their own protection is also an act of defiance against the fatalistic understanding that one day it may be their own turn to kill or be killed. While accepting that the dangers are very real and near, the night commuter children fight with the limited resources available to them.

An additional act of defiance is that most of the night commuter children continue to go to school in spite of the hardships they face and their physical and emotional exhaustion. The children rise early after what has likely been an uncomfortable night and make their way to school. Few will have any breakfast. Often they attempt to do homework at the shelters before going to sleep. Although their very lives have been interrupted by the threat of the LRA, they are determined to continue to receive an education, but it is not easy.

One young girl who displays this determination was fourteen years old when she was interviewed by IRIN in January 2004.[1] Prossy, who was living with her grandmother in Paicho, ten kilometers from Gulu, explained how she was valiantly continuing school as a night commuter, though she said she was tired of walking without eating.

My father was killed by the rebels in 1996. My mother died in 1998 after a long illness.

I walk every evening to the Noah's Ark centre in Gulu town. I go to school each morning with nothing to eat. During the fruit season, you can get something to eat during the day, but now there are no fruits, so the only time I eat is in the evening when I go home from school. I have to eat very quickly so as to leave home before dark. Sometimes when the situation gets worse, I have to hurry to reach the centre before dark. At times I do not wait to eat at home. I do not want to end up like my sister, who was abducted in 1994. I don't think she is alive. We have not heard anything about her from other children who have come back.

164

Another young girl, Lilian, eleven years old, was in school when interviewed, but she doubted she could continue into secondary school with no support.

The rebels first abducted my brother in 1997. He has never come back. We don't know where he is. I don't think he is alive, because I have not heard any reports about him from other children who have come back. This year, one of my elder brothers and two younger sisters were also abducted on the same night. None of them has returned. Both my parents have died. I don't remember when they died—I was still very small. My aunt adopted me. I was told rebels came home and murdered them.

I am only left with two brothers. We all come to Noah's Ark every evening. In the morning, we leave for school. There is no feeding program in our school. Even in schools which have feeding programs, parents still have to pay for the food, salt, onions and firewood.

No, I don't think of the future. I don't think I'll go to secondary school. There is no one to help. All my relatives are very poor now because of this war. They are all scattered in camps. Rebels killed some of them. My aunt is very ill. She can't do anything but cook.

Few Social Restraints Protect Girls

Besides fear of rebels, the girls and women who commute are particularly vulnerable to sexual predators. Girl and women night commuters frequently report sexual harassment and abuse as they travel to the town center and sometimes in the shelters. Beyond the sexual assaults themselves, the risks of contracting HIV/AIDS, contracting other sexually transmitted diseases and becoming pregnant in a rape is very real for young night commuter girls. In a situation where there are no other alternatives, commuting is still safer than remaining in the village or the camp, exposed to LRA attack.

As many as 25,000 were leaving their home villages or the displacement camps in Gulu District and walking into town, according to the Tear Fund, a relief agency representing several churches and groups in the United Kingdom.[2] Fortunate ones stay at places such as Noah's Ark, one of the largest night commuter centers in northern Uganda. At this shelter, children are expected to arrive by 7 P.M. Sleeping space for boys and girls is kept separate, giving an extra measure of security to vulnerable girls. The shelter also provides a bath as well as the opportunity to participate in such activities as singing, drama, health discussions, debates, praying and Bible study. From sundown until morning, several UPDF soldiers are stationed outside the shelter.

A delegation from the Women's Commission for Refugee Women and Children that visited the shelter discovered that Noah's Ark had become greatly overcrowded with "children at times literally sleeping on top of one another." Other children slept on the veranda outside the main shelter.[3]

One of the social workers at Noah's Ark, Emanuel, expressed concern for the children who were staying out on the veranda:

Our biggest concern is their behaviour. Those who sleep on the verandahs are becoming spoiled. They think there are good things on the street. On the street, they are free to do what they want. They watch videos and all sorts of things which are not good. This means that the number of children on the verandahs is growing every day, because more and more children prefer the free life in town. They are ruining their future. There has to be a way of getting off the street or there will be no future.[4]

Those who cannot fit into Noah's Ark, which in June of 2004 was sheltering as many as six thousand children each night, have to stay in one of the other twelve district-designated sleeping centers in Gulu. These are more makeshift shelters on the grounds of hospitals, schools, shop verandas and bus parks. The local police in Gulu are supposed to make sure that night commuters all go to the shelters, but they often harass the children. UPDF soldiers and drunken civilians also have been accused of mistreating the children.

A survey conducted by the Women's Commission for Refugee Women and Children in December 2003 revealed that over twenty-one thousand night commuters were sleeping in the town center of Kitgum each night. Twelve locations were listed, with up to eight thousand each at St. Joseph's Hospital and Kitgum Government Hospital; three thousand at the Justro Pastore School; and hundreds each at the Ministry of Works, Kitgum Public School, other government administration locations, shop verandas, the bus park and the Uganda Martyrs Center.[5]

The Women's Commission for Refugee Women and Children was concerned because the provisions for the night commuters made by the Kitgum District government officials were not as comprehensive and structured as those in Gulu. "This lack of support has led to difficult and often chaotic and dangerous sleeping conditions for the nightly displaced in Kitgum," the Women's Commission report warns.[6]

St. Joseph's Hospital has managed to provide some structure and supervision for the children. The hospital has created seven temporary shelters for night commuters, but overflow means that many children sleep on the verandas and under the open sky. Children who come unaccompanied by adults are sent to sleep in boy-only or girl-only shelters. They are required to go to the same shelter each night and not to move between shelters. In addition, at St. Joseph's Mission Hospital, teams patrol and help to supervise the night commuters. Most other shelters do not have the facilities or personnel to provide these services.

Nothing for the Night Commuters

Sometimes not even the most basic services are provided to the night commuters in Kitgum. The Women's Commission follow-up report says that the children at all of the sleeping spaces in Kitgum reported that there was not enough clean water or latrines. Without any financial assistance or tax credits from the Kitgum District government, many of the facilities have had to shut off water and electricity to the night commuters. In addition, some children at Kitgum Public School reported having to pay for water, electricity and trash removal. Those at Kitgum Government Hospital said that they had to pay for candles.

Cornelius Williams, the UNICEF protection officer and field coordinator for Kitgum District, has remarked, "The night commuters should not be expected to pay for basic amenities in the night commuter spaces when they are forced out of their homes. It is the government's responsibility to provide for those needs."[7]

The government should be providing security for the night commuters. The district government in Kitgum has not provided adequate security for the vulnerable children who must walk to Kitgum. There is insufficient light on the roads as the children travel, and many must leave after night has fallen. There are not enough proper police and other security personnel. Security is left up to unarmed volunteers who cannot prevent abuse to the night commuters. Night commuters have testified that, although they feel safer when they are inside Kitgum town, they feel threatened both along the way and in the sleeping centers. Night commuters have, at times, been abducted by the LRA when making their way back to the IDP camp after spending the night in Kitgum. The Women's Commission advises that district officials should examine the conditions for night commuters, both en route and inside each of the Kitgum sleeping centers, to provide the needed security.[8]

IRIN reports that LRA rebels have tried to gain access to the sleep centers. Geoffrey, a social worker from St. Joseph's Mission Hospital, described the need for vigilance and the lack of support from the Ugandan military in a January 2004 report:

We have to make sure that rebels do not infiltrate the compound. A few days ago, we caught four rebels with guns tucked inside their blankets. We know each and every face that enters this compound. If you don't watch out, then the LRA can easily infiltrate and abduct people from here. You can say it is only God who is protecting us here. The UPDF are here, but we don't see them and we have no communication with them. If the rebels come, we have to run and look for them.[9]

Maranatha Children's Center is a shelter for three thousand night commuters fifteen miles outside of Kitgum. The center was built and operated by Far Reaching Ministries, an American Christian agency directed by Wes Bentley. Maranatha Center is a fortified compound, encircled by fences topped with razor wire and protected by armed guards, but they also have had problems with attacks by the LRA. Bentley told journalist J. Carter Johnson that the center had been attacked by the LRA while they were building it. "We couldn't get it up fast enough, so many people were seeking protection at night," said Bentley in Johnson's article.[10]

God's Gift of Defiance

There is a defiant set of the thin shoulders among the children who make their way into town with whatever meager belongings they have to help them get through the night. The defiance shows even when those shoulders are stooped in despair and depression. There is defiance deep in their eyes, even though the beautiful brown eyes that should flash with spirit and humor are dulled by fear and monotony. There is defiance in the strong, high, clear voices that can still laugh or sing sweet songs while a symphony of evil is circling their heads.

This defiance has not been lost in many children because it is a gift from God. It is the strengthening of a child's will and the ability to persevere that comes from His unseen, and maybe unfelt, embrace. It is His Holy Spirit that whispers to a child's spirit, "You are not invisible to Me. I am your Protector."

Some northern Ugandan children are very aware that their courage to go on, their defiance in the face of devastation, comes from the Lord. Others may only know that there is something that keeps them going when they are tired. Many things exhaust these children—war, running from abduction, sleeping on the ground in the rain, walking without eating, being set upon by other children or the adults that should protect them and trying to concentrate on studies at a sleeping center. The children are tired of trying to survive.

NBC *Dateline* correspondent Keith Morrison was sent to northern Uganda in August 2005. After meeting and reporting on the night commuters and abducted children who had returned, Morrison said that he left Uganda a changed man. "When we visited one of the refugee camps I found myself wondering how long I would survive in one of them," Morrison confessed. "A few days? A week? It's humbling to realize how soft life is in the West—how tough these people are."[11]

But it was not just the toughness, the resilience that impressed Morrison. He caught a glimpse of the grace-filled defiance:

And then we saw the night commuters. So strange and sad. They were little kids—5, 6 years old. There were teenagers, rowdy boys, mothers with brand new babies. The kids had gone to school all day, then walked for miles and miles just for the chance to sleep safely where the rebels can't kidnap them. They filled up tents set up by Doctors Without Borders and other groups. They filled up city schools, libraries, enclosed courtyards, any available safe place. We asked some of them, how often do you eat? Once a day, they told us. They drink dirty water. Most of them are at risk of dying from malaria and other diseases the rest of us could cure with one trip to the drugstore. They have no shoes.

But you hang out around one of the sleeping centers and they look up at you and laugh and laugh. They chatter, dance, organize games, tell jokes.

Even while they deal with horrors so vile they are beyond imagining. As I say, you come back changed.[12]

Carolyn Davis, a member of the editorial board of *The Philadelphia Inquirer*, had an even more profound experience with the grace and defiance given to the Acholi children. In the paradoxical way in which God sometimes works, Davis had a crisis of faith that arose when she worked in Rwanda for UNICEF. Yet her faith was strengthened when she went to northern Uganda. From Kitgum, she wrote:

I didn't expect to feel healed when I came to Uganda to see firsthand a situation I have followed for more than a decade: a civil war in which about 30,000 children have been abducted to serve as soldiers or sex slaves. I didn't expect to have my cracked faith spackled while spending a night watching the fitful sleep of children whom I consider to be the most victimized in the world—and the most ignored.

But I did and it was.[13]

While "staying up all night and watching a bunch of kids sleep," Davis pondered over the inconceivable reality that the war had been going on for nineteen years and "the world had not come to these children's rescue." She heard the rain and felt the same cold and hunger "that squeezes so many in northern Uganda." She heard what she thought might be gunfire and experienced "the vulnerability of living in a war zone."[14] She continued:

It was early in the night, when I began to feel different, when I realized the cracks that had appeared in Rwanda were gone. My crisis of faith was replaced by a stronger-still belief in God. I tried to rationalize why and how that moment had happened amid a human tragedy. Maybe it was seeing the children laugh, play and share their possessions with others despite their situation.

Maybe it was an inexpressibly satisfying feeling that at least for one night, I could help protect them, that I was acting on my concern for these kids.

Maybe it was all that and other reasons too. But after my night commute, I don't care anymore about dissecting what happened. Now, having faith that it did is enough.[15]

19

Learning to Live without a Gun

grace:

"God had not brought us this far only to kill us."

Our guns were still strapped onto our backs, because a gun meant life. Without it there was no life in the LRA. After crossing the water and walking for a long time, there was a whisper in my heart, telling me that if we kept the guns we would get killed.

I was learning to listen to this gentle voice that spoke to my heart. This time what was said was hard to accept. I didn't know how I would convince my friends to throw away what seemed to be their last hope. The voice would not leave me alone. It continued to whisper in my ears to drop the guns.

"Let us throw these guns away, and we will be safe," I told the girls as if speaking to myself.

The girls looked at me like I was a stranger who had emerged from the bush and was ready to shoot at them.

"If we drop the guns, we will be safe," I repeated.

There was no answer. They just continued to look at me. I wondered whether they had heard me at all. The gun was life. It was used for protection and getting food from the local people, both in Sudan and Uganda.

I was asking them to drop their lives.

Agnes was a little bit older than the rest of us, and she had lived with the Lord's Resistance Army longer. She had a more commanding voice than the rest of us, and now she yelled at me, "Have you lost your mind? You know very well that without guns we are defenseless." Agnes almost convinced me. She was right. Without a gun, we were defenseless. But I was also sure that if we met civilians from Sudan, they would believe we had come to attack them. They would call on the SPLA to help them.

My friends listened to Agnes. I was losing my strength again, but with great power I asked, "Do you think those guns will protect you? Why did you run away? Why don't you go back to the camp? Why didn't guns save us when we had no way of crossing the water? If you cannot throw your guns, then go. No one should follow me holding a gun. Unless you are going to shoot me, which I doubt, then you go right now."

They were all silent; I had taken control of the group again.

"Who is that?" one girl whispered as she moved to the nearest tree to hide. We all looked in the direction she had pointed. Two women carrying baggage on their heads were talking loudly, and stopping to hear gunshots behind them. They were running from the same fighting we had run from.

"I am going to call," I said, getting up. Miriam, one of the girls, pulled me down so that the women would not see me. I got up again. It was the right thing to do. I called to them. When the women heard my voice, they threw down their baggage and raced away from us like a lion was chasing them. All was quiet except the pounding of their feet. When I turned back to my friends to say I was sorry, they had disappeared into hiding. I saw only the tips of their guns pointing in the direction the women had taken. I laughed out loud not because of joy but because I had nothing to do. I had tried my best to follow the voice in me and tried to convince myself that we would be rescued, but everything was backfiring.

"Come out. The women have fled," I said to the girls peering from the grass. It took a little while before they came out. It was going to be hard to convince them to throw away their AK-47 machine guns. They came out with eyes darting all around, ready to dash back in case of attack.

"What is your plan?" Agnes asked as she was coming out of the small depression she had managed to fit her bony body into.

"We should throw the guns," I answered her.

"No, we are not going to throw our guns. You saw what just happened. Those women are going to report us, and we will be attacked," Agnes rumbled. The others nodded in agreement as usual.

"We will be killed if we keep the guns," I told them. They would not listen to me, so I told them to go back.

Susan, who was about twelve years old, looked at me as if she was trying to find the truth. She said, "I am going with you." The others could not believe their ears, but they said nothing.

"Very well, then you others can go back if you don't want to drop your guns," I said. I covered my gun with the dry grass and started to walk away. Susan did the same and followed me.

"Where are you from?" I asked her as she walked beside me. "Pabor," she answered. "I was captured on the way home from school. They told me to lead them home. If I didn't they would kill me, and I did. They killed my parents in front of me, beating them with heavy sticks until they died." As Susan opened up to me, her eyes were misty with tears. I had no strength to hold her and tell her that things would be fine. Our lives were at stake, and we didn't know if we would live. I was deep in thought.

I turned and was surprised to see the whole group behind us, with no guns. They had thrown them away. *This is God, not me,* I thought. We walked quietly. I never asked a question about it, but I was glad they came. They had become my friends.

At around 6 P.M., after walking for four days, we entered a settled land. For the first time I saw a boy tending sheep in the bush. I thought we were safe, but that was not the case. I decided to call the boy, but he jumped and disappeared. We were left with the sheep, and they didn't understand what was going on. Soon they also raced in the direction the boy had gone. We could not get help, and we didn't know how to survive in this dry land. Even the sheep were ready to run for their dear lives when they saw us. We were left wondering what to do.

My friends started to run, but I told them not to. It was too late, and if they did I would scream. I only wanted help and had no strength to run again. Enough was enough. I was ready for anything. I told my friends to raise their hands in surrender and shout in our local language that we were not bad people. We had been abducted from Uganda and some of us from school, and I shouted in the little English I knew. I was just learning to speak English in school, but my memory of it was disappearing. Among the rebels we were not allowed to speak English.

Forward we moved in a single line, me in the front, shouting:
"We are not bad people."

"We were abducted, some of us from school."

"We need your help, please."

We shouted like that until we reached a clearing that had
a shelter. It was the home of this boy we had seen tending the
sheep. There were signs that people were here. The boy had
surely alerted people about us. My friends were almost giving
up, but I encouraged them to continue shouting. I sensed that
people were hiding and trying to see whether we were armed.
We shouted for almost an hour. Then soldiers in uniform came
running toward us. They were shouting, but we didn't understand what they were saying, we just continued to lift our hands.
My friends started to run when the soldiers neared us. I had
no control over them now. I was gripped by fear also, yet I did
not move. I believed God had not brought us this far only to
kill us.

The soldiers rushed to capture my friends. They brought them
back to where I was standing and tied cloth over our eyes. I was
just waiting for the bullet that would blow apart my head; I was
tired, tired of living. I was so tired I didn't want to face another day.
Everything had come to a standstill. I was ready for my fate.

But the voice that had led me to this place whispered again,
telling me to say that we were not bad people but we needed
help.

"We are not bad people."

"We need your help . . . please."

I repeated the words aloud, and with shock I felt someone
touch my shoulder and tell me to repeat the words. I did, and
he translated them to the group of soldiers who were ready to
shoot us. I could hear a commotion. The last thing I expected

happened. The man uncovered our faces and started to plead for us. He was trying to cover us with his body, raising his hands in front of us. He pleaded until the soldiers dropped their guns and sat down.

An old man hurried to make some porridge for us. He told us to take it and be prepared to walk for eight kilometers to the Sudan People's Liberation Army barracks. I did not care about the walking; I had been doing that since I was abducted.

We took our porridge and started our trekking again in single line, with soldiers behind and in front of us. We reached the barracks at around 11 P.M., and I was chosen to be taken to their leader. He looked me in the eyes and asked if I understood English. I just nodded to him.

He told me that they were going to keep us for a week, monitoring us closely to make sure we were not spies sent to find their position.

We stayed in the barracks for a week. There was no problem until a gang of boys from this barracks attempted to rape us. They entered the shelter where my friends were sleeping. I was outside. I was used to sleeping with no shelter. I heard the screams and shouted at the boys. They came out, pretending there had been an attack, and they were making sure we had not escaped.

They waited until I had fallen asleep again and went back inside, but I woke up before they did anything to my friends. I shouted, and another boy who was sleeping nearby in camp woke up and came to my aid. He ordered his friends out. The next morning they were reported to their leader, and we were taken to another barracks.

In the second barracks, I was the one who was almost raped. A boy followed when we went to the second barracks. He called me to his shelter. I went, thinking he wanted to tell me something since I was the only one who could speak a little English. Instead he ordered me to remove my clothes and said he would shoot me if I did not do it.

This boy is joking, I thought. *I have passed through the fire, and he thinks I will be afraid and just obey him.*

"Remove your clothes," he screamed at me.

"No," I said.

"Do you see these?" he said, pointing at his gun and knife. He pulled me down, but I grabbed the knife from him and told him to hand the gun to me. I put the knife blade to his stomach. There was no way he was going to get his gun around and shoot me. I took the gun, too, and just walked out. I handed the gun and knife to their leader. From that time, the boy never came near me, but he convinced his friends to come and threaten me and the girls. I stood my ground.

We were taken away from that barracks and carried on top of a tank with cans of petrol to the base of John Garang, the head of the SPLA rebellion against the government of Sudan. When we reached this place, we were frightened to see a deep pit with many dead bodies in it. They forced us to go down into the pit with these dead bodies. They did not kill us, but we had to live for awhile with the dead. After some time, soldiers came to take me away. My friends thought I was going to be killed. Since I saved them from the boys in the barracks, my friends had called me "mammy." Now they tried to pull me away from the person who had come to take me. I told them it would be okay; God was in control.

"Who are you?" asked a bearded man who was sitting on a stool as soon as I came to him. I didn't know I was talking to the rebel leader Garang. I told him how I had been abducted from school in Uganda. "My friends and I need your help," I said.

He looked at me, then told his escorts to pull the other girls from the pit and give us some food. He then told me that they were going to hand us over to the Ugandan soldiers who were fighting alongside them. That very day a car came and took us away.

My heart sank when I saw that the car had brought us back to the very same place where we had escaped from Kony. I thought we were being given back to him. But now the SPLA had taken over the camp, and Ugandan soldiers were there.

"Are there any Aboke girls among you?" one soldier asked. I had grown tired of that name, which had meant only fear for me. So I kept quiet, but my friends answered that there was and pointed at me. The soldier told me to follow him. I thought they were going to kill me because I was from Aboke. I had come to the point where I did not trust anyone.

He took me to a man who looked like an Arab. He had light skin. I thought only the Arabs had light skin.

"Where are you from, and what are you doing here?" he asked me.

I just looked at him, then said, "Sir, I am very hungry. If you give me food, maybe I can tell who I am and where I am from."

The man nodded and told an aide to give me water for a bath and food to eat. They were also to help my friends. When he did this, I knew I was safe. I had survived and was going to see my family again.

We were transported to Uganda, and we stayed at a Ugandan army base for a night. The next day my friends were taken to World Vision. It was the first time I had heard of World Vision. I was taken to the main army barracks.

My tears rolled freely. I hadn't cried since the day of my abduction except when I was praying. Other than that, my eyes were always dry. But this day my tears flowed freely with relief when I saw Sister Rachele hurrying toward me with her hands open to hug me. I was still weak, but I gathered my little strength and ran to her. She made me feel safe. We cried, and she asked me about the others.

I had no way to know whether they were alive because everybody had gone in different directions when the camp was attacked. Now I knew that I was alive but not free because of my friends. I had left them in that hell.

20

The Adults Are Not Around

> "Night commuter children exist where none of the usual moral values and societal inhibitions are in place."

One problem for the night commuters in Kitgum is caused by gangs of boys. Children, shelter administrators and watchmen all reported that these boys, sometimes accompanied by adult men, are a major source of violent disturbance at sleeping centers. The boys and men come to the shelters in a drunken state from a nearby disco. They terrorize small children, stealing their blankets and sleeping mats. They reportedly have raped girl night commuters. Watchmen and other adults, including the shelter staff, have been threatened by the gangs and attacked with stones.

Richard, a twelve-year-old boy at the Kitgum Primary School sleeping center, told of his experience with these older bullies:

There are always gangs of boys who come here. I had my blanket stolen by some of them. They also hit us with stones. Yesterday a ten-year-old boy was hit hard in the head with a stone. I went to the security guard, but he did nothing to help. He was afraid. Last month I was beaten up too. The older boys hit me with a stone here on my head. The next morning I went to my father who took me to the hospital. Now I just try and hide whenever the gangs come into the school.[1]

The administrators at Kitgum Primary School and at Kitgum Government Hospital both reported that they had submitted a request for assistance with security to the local authorities, including both the civil authority and the military, but they had received no reply at the time of the Women's Commission report.[2]

According to IRIN, in both Gulu and Kitgum, some people who started out as nightly commuters have stopped going home altogether. In Gulu, it has been mostly night commuter children who do not go home anymore because life in their communities is too hard and too dangerous. They stay in town and earn a little money to survive by cleaning buses or helping to sell food in the marketplace.[3]

In Kitgum, hundreds of children and adults set up camp for the day under a huge mango tree outside the gates of St. Joseph's Mission Hospital. From there they go off in search of odd jobs and return to the hospital in midafternoon. It could be that it is just easier to stay in town and be assured of a good sleeping spot, or perhaps "home" is not what it used to be. One group in Kitgum has stayed on since May 2003 when the rebels burned their camp. "We have been displaced too many times," the former night commuters now staying in Kitgum said. "We have nothing. We are traumatized. We have lost faith in the ability of the government to protect us."[4]

Sexual Issues among Commuters

Wherever there are night commuters, there are potential problems with sexual harassment and rape. Johnson discovered that girls walking into town are frequently sexually abused by boy night commuters or drunken men in town. Girls and women told members of the Women's Commission that adolescent boys and young men from their own communities had molested or raped them. These include boda boda boys, who wait at corners and sell rides on bicycles. Some also named UPDF soldiers as rapists and said that both the soldiers and some of the boys were armed. Incidents of rape and sexual harassment that take place just outside of and even within the shelters have also been reported.[5]

The testimony of one young girl night commuter to Kitgum is an example of why many girls are especially vulnerable to sexual abuse. "Lizzy," a fifteen-year-old commuter from Pamoro, explains that some commuters travel to town late because of home responsibilities:

> I am in S2 at Kitgum Town College, and I live in Làbuje IDP camp near town. I am an orphan. I have come to St. Joseph's Hospital three to four times per week to sleep for the past three months. I usually arrive by 8 P.M. There is a problem near Kitgum Boys School. I see the same boys, a group of about five of them, bothering me and other girls at the same place every night. Girls need to leave earlier, in daylight, to increase our security. I also think police should patrol schools where abuses take place.
>
> Other girls and I often walk alone for several reasons. Many times our parents remain behind, and those who are orphans like me have no one to accompany us. I lost both parents, and earlier this year, I also lost my elder brother when he was killed by the LRA. As an orphan, I receive help to continue my education, al-

though most young people at Labuje are unable to attend school. After school, I must prepare my dinner, which takes a lot of time, and I cook for others. I normally sleep on a piece of ground just in front of a covered verandah where others sleep. When it rains, others and I stand under the verandah, and we do not rest well. As the day breaks, I walk alongside others and head home.[6]

Many girls are required to do household chores, cook dinner for their parents and do other activities that cause them to leave for town later. Some have reported that their parents promise to accompany them. Then, after the girls wait for them, the parents decide not to go, leaving the girls to get there on their own. Others promise to follow but never show up, again leaving the girls to decide where to sleep. Parents who place their children in such danger are frequently those who drink a lot of alcohol.

Emanuel, the social worker at Noah's Ark shelter in Gulu, confirms these problems. "The parents are not serious about taking responsibility," he says. "They are not checking to make sure that their children are where they are supposed to be." It is the parents' responsibility to find out if the children have reached their sleeping place, but Emanuel relays that all many parents are concerned about is where to get food. Others, he says, "are totally traumatized by the war and have become drunkards."[7]

Ronald Opira, the director of a youth advocacy organization called Watwero Rights Focus Initiative, working for improved security for the night commuters, expressed outrage over the abuse of girls by soldiers in testimony to the Women's Commission:

I spoke with a group of children at St. Joseph's Mission Hospital. They explained that last night they had watched several Local Defense Unit soldiers try to attack three girls just outside the hospital. Some of the children who were walking nearby started to run in all directions. The girls managed to run away during the confusion. The three soldiers ran off too. The children told me that they could identify the girls if I needed them to.

The children reported to me that the soldiers had been hiding behind some large trees on the road that comes up to the hospital gate. This road is very dark and has many places for people to hide. The Labuje IDP camp is also nearby, so there are many LDU soldiers with guns nearby as well. I plan to talk to the security officer at the district council about the dark road to the hospital and the soldiers who are causing these problems.

The soldiers are supposed to be here to protect us, not to attack young girls. The police are not doing enough either to watch out for the young ones.[8]

Arriving unscathed at the sleeping center does not guarantee an unmolested night. In Kitgum, girls worry, with good reason, about the "mixed" sleeping space. Shelters like those at Kitgum Government Hospital lack adequate support and organization to offer separate sleeping space for males and females. This provides opportunities for boys to take advantage of girls, knowing that many of them will never report being raped because of the societal stigma.

Four young night commuter girls reported to the Women's Commission team that the hospital was not secure, and there was not enough light. "We do not have separate sleeping spaces, and boys often try to sleep near us," they said. "We would prefer a separate sleeping space, even if it were with the old women." They said that boys often tried to "force themselves on girls" while they were sleeping.[9]

Night commuter children exist where none of the usual moral values and societal inhibitions are in place. Cowardly, wicked men, such as the soldier rapists and other abusive adults, have few constraints and face little chance of punishment if they take advantage of the vulnerable. These are not normal circumstances.

Some of the boys have more complicated explanations as to why they attack girls. A team of male interviewers from the Women's Commission asked night commuter boys about the situation. They discovered that "the breakdown of traditional courtship customs and spaces has caused some boys to become more aggressive in their interaction with girls." Under normal circumstances, a boy would have to seek the approval of a girl's parents before courting her. He would have to provide assurance that he could support the girl financially. But under the current circumstances, none of this is possible. Boys report that the lack of opportunity for employment "has also made it too embarrassing for adolescent boys to approach the parents of girls they want to get to know."[10]

One older night commuter boy, David from Labuje IDP camp, gave the same reason for the mistreatment of girls by night commuters and other boys:

> I know of older boys that rape and menace girls when they come into town. I don't agree with what they do, but I do understand that they feel lots of pressure to meet girls. We used to have places we could go and talk to girls we found pretty. Eventually we would go to their parents asking if it was okay to marry their daughter. Those traditional places and customs are gone now. The war has made it very difficult to interact with girls.
>
> Without a place to meet girls, boys are forced to meet girls in other ways. Some boys think that, because so many girls are on the road at night, this is a good opportunity to talk to them. The girls dress in "revealing" clothing, so some boys think that the girls want to be approached. I don't agree with this, but when you don't have a job and have very little money, how can you

approach a girl or her parents to tell them that you are interested in their daughter?

I feel lots of pressure from other boys to approach girls on the road and in the dark. They tell me that it is okay to force a girl to "love" me, but I don't agree. We should have a fun place where we can talk to girls. We need jobs, too, so that we can feel confident enough to approach a girl's parents. These boys who rape girls are breaking a lot of traditional values of our people. Normally village leaders would punish them, but with this war, the adults are not around to promote our traditional values.[11]

Since adults are not around to teach values, younger boys look to the older adolescents as role models. Unfortunately, not all of the older boys are as mature and self-controlled as the young man above. Watwero director Ronald Opira said that he heard a group of older boys tell a group of girls and younger boys that it was okay to harass the girls. "They were saying it is okay to force girls to love them," Opira reported. He was very worried about this, particularly since they had been bold enough to declare that they were going to force the girls "'to love them tonight.' This is not a good example for the younger boys who look up to them," said Opira.[12]

The younger boys told Opira that the older boys who had been speaking and acting in this way attended Kitgum Public School. He discovered that these boys returned to the school every night "just to choose which girls they want to 'love.'" Opira met with the school administrators, and for a time, the boys no longer bothered girls at the sleeping center. The follow-up visit by the Women's Commission the next year, though, revealed that gangs of boys were back.[13]

21

Finding Life Again

grace:

> "There is no future without healthy
> children who grow up in a peaceful
> environment."

You have read the true story about my life when I was dragged into the bush like an animal. After a long struggle, surviving on leaves and soil, I reached safety on Good Friday 1997. I was in captivity for exactly seven months, and when I escaped I left behind my friends. Even though I was safe, I felt dry, like a branch plucked from the tree.

I again enrolled in high school at St. Mary's College, Aboke, and graduated in 2001. I had the opportunity then to go on to Uganda Christian University at Mukono, majoring in mass communication. My dream was beginning to come true, though I no longer wanted to study to be a lawyer. My life was not the same. I hated war and prayed for all people who go through war.

At St. Mary's College, I felt helpless. I felt guilty that I had left my friends behind, though I knew there was nothing I could have done. Pain settled in my heart. It was a deep wound with no medicine to cure it.

I was afraid to meet the parents of my friends. There would always be questions about what happened to their children, for which I had no answers. Their eyes were always watery from crying. It was more pain than I could bear. Everywhere I went, it seemed that something reminded me of the suffering I had gone through. It was far from over, but one thing I knew was that God was going to rescue my friends, and I prayed for them as never before. I could pray at any time, even while putting food in my mouth. I did blame God for letting this happen, and yet I praised Him for rescuing me.

No person could rescue my friends, but God could—just as He had rescued me.

Telling Our Story to the World

In 2002, while I was at Uganda Christian University, a journalist was brought to me by Els De Temmerman, the author of *Aboke Girls: Children Abducted in Northern Uganda*.[1] Henk Rossouw, a South African, was not the first journalist I had met since my release. Many came to write stories about our abduction, but nothing changed. My friends were still under the claws of a lion. I came to the point that I didn't want to talk about it because nothing came of it. Sister Rachele also was going from one place to another, pleading with people to help.

Henk wrote a story about me and some of my friends who had managed to escape. It appeared on the front page of the *Chronicle of Higher Education.*[2] Someone with Amnesty International U.S.A. read it, and they invited me to speak at their annual meeting in New York City. Perhaps God was sending me to speak for the poor children who are dragged every day into the wild.

I arrived in New York after my first time on an airplane. My first time in the United States began in New York City, the best-known city in the world. I only knew of New York City on the map, but suddenly I was landing there, and I would stay for a few days.

Jason, a missionary to Uganda and professor at Uganda Christian University, came to meet me, but his car had broken down so he soon had to leave to check on it. Someone from Amnesty International would pick me up. So I waited, looking around at the busy airport and wondering if someone was asking for me. Then a stranger with dark hair approached. "Are you Grace?" she asked. I looked straight at her face. Some moments passed. "Yes," I said slowly. Then she hugged me and started chatting as she took me to the hotel.

Brooklyn Hotel looked like a place for executives on the outside. The outside made me want to see the inside part immediately. Inside it was cool and welcoming, and Elise, my host, took me to my room. The room was large with a big bed for two people and two telephones. I had never slept in such a place before, but here I was, sleeping like a president, only remembering that my friends and many other children had nothing to eat.

I was determined to speak to anyone who would listen and might help. On April 16, 2004, I spoke earnestly at the meeting, as if the lives of my friends depended on the outcome of that one speech. I was determined not to cry but to pour everything out.

Two days later, I flew to Chicago to be on *The Oprah Winfrey Show* on television. (In the United States, this is a popular daily program, on which Oprah Winfrey interviews people on many topics.) My new journey to represent the children of war had begun. I had to be at the studio at seven in the morning, but my flight wasn't to arrive until two hours later. A special flight was arranged for me at 4:30 A.M. I was amazed that this could be accomplished.

I left for Chicago, thanking God that I was accompanied by my host, Elise. At the airport in Chicago, I saw a man holding a paper with my name on it. Elise and I went to the man, who took us to a long, black car that was waiting for us. I had never seen such a car. The air in the car was cool, and everything was inside. Only the president has a limousine in Uganda, and I had not seen it. I was received by a woman named Kettie for a pre-interview at the very large studio.

April 21 was the day of the actual interview. I was going to see the famous Oprah Winfrey face-to-face. I waited backstage with anxiety, ready to tell the world and put the children of northern Uganda on the map for millions of people. I heard yelling and shouting but did not know what was going on. "Oprah is coming," someone in the crowd yelled. Everyone got up and started clapping their hands. I didn't clap my hands. I wanted to see her. At last she came. She was beautiful. "Oprah, you are skinny," a voice called from the back. People know that she works hard to be skinny. The show was about giving children who are voiceless a voice. She started by interviewing a girl who had been sent against her will from Africa to the United States by sex traffickers. She also interviewed a film producer.

It was my turn. My heart was racing. I was excited that the whole world was going to hear my message. She asked me to tell how I was abducted, how I came back and where I now lived. I told the story, and Oprah shouted, "Get up. The world wants to see you. You are a great lady." The people were quiet. There was no coughing and much shaking of heads. I felt that they heard me and were concerned and would act to help the situation. I looked at this audience as representing the world.

After that I went to schools and spoke to children about what is going on in Uganda.

Back home again, I returned to Uganda Christian University and earned my diploma in 2004. I wanted to continue my studies, but I did not know where to get money. God was with me, and I got a scholarship from Uganda Christian University to continue with my degree. Then I met exchange students from Gordon College, Wenham, Massachusetts. Interacting with them, I loved what they said about their school. I decided to apply and was admitted. I was given a full scholarship to cover tuition, and Uganda Partners paid for board, food and health insurance. As I write these words, I am a student at Gordon College and will be finished by the time people read this book, in May 2007.

While I have been in school, I have not been able to do a lot directly for the people of northern Uganda. I am frequently invited to speak, and I tell my story and the story of the Acholi and of the need for peace whenever I can.

In April of 2006, I had the opportunity to tell the U.S. government personally about northern Uganda. I was invited by World Vision to testify at hearings before members of the U.S. House of Representatives' International Relations Committee. The Subcommittee on Africa, Global Human Rights and International Operations convened hearings on my speech "The Endangered

Children of Northern Uganda." The hearings were organized by Representative Adam Smith (D-Wash.).[3]

I have been very happy to work with World Vision International. World Vision is one of the organizations working effectively in Uganda to help the children find their lives again. I have been at World Vision's Rehabilitation Center to visit some friends who came back after me. I have also volunteered at Rachele Rehabilitation Center, which was started by Els De Temmerman, the Belgian woman who wrote *Aboke Girls*.

For the Children of War

I have seen heads smashed. I have seen people beaten until their sockets swallow their eyes. I have survived being buried alive. After over twenty years of pain in my land, I ache for peace. I remember the painful look of the young children I left behind, some as young as seven years old. I still cannot go to sleep at night without a thought about these poor children. I wish I had wings. I would fly to them and carry them on my bosom to safety. I did not deserve the freedom I have now more than they, but there is a purpose for my freedom.

I am not sure what I will do with the degree in mass communications I am finishing in the United States. I would like to go to graduate school and study international relations and conflict resolution, but I do not know if that will be possible. I do know that I have been given these great gifts so that I can tell others about the need for peace. That is the main message I talk about when I go around the United States. Our war has been going on a very long time. We need peace so that we can go back home. The people need the world to give them a future.

The Acholi have a history of Christian faith, although it has gotten all mixed up with tribal religions. But many have been praying, and God has helped them to be strong. There is nothing else they can depend on now but God.

The problem is that they don't understand why God has allowed them to go through what they have. They believe they are being punished for something. They don't know God's love and mercy.

Living in the camps, without work or a way to grow much food, causes all of life to revolve around surviving. Most marriages fall apart, so children are raised by their mothers alone. The fathers go off and don't return because they don't know how to provide for their families. Mothers spend their energy trying to find food, so there is no parenting of the children. They haven't had the blessing I had of a community and a family and a grandfather who told stories around the fire.

To those who read this book, I want you to pray for the children who are at this moment going through hell on earth. They deserve a future. I am speaking not just of the children in northern Uganda but all the little ones who are caught in the midst of war. To the companies who manufacture arms and sell them to the people who destroy the creation of God, stop and look at your child. Picture him or her dragged into the swamp and forest against his or her will.

To the whole world, this is my cry: There is no future without healthy children who grow up in a peaceful environment. Do not turn your hatred on the children.

22

Hearts Full of Northern Uganda

faith:

> "The builders of the protection of love are
> defiant in the face of the deception that
> says, 'There is nothing you can do.'"

Who is protecting the children of northern Uganda? They are making their own protection, but even as they do, God is watching over them. God's intervention to save the children of northern Uganda is evident today in many ways and many circumstances. Sometimes the circumstances were miraculous, as they were with Grace Akallo.

Isaiah 59:15–16 says, "The LORD looked and was displeased that there was no justice. He saw that there was no one, he was appalled that there was no one to intervene; so his own arm worked salvation for him." God's hand was over Grace Akallo through the darkest and most dangerous of her days, even as she wondered if there was anyone to protect her.

The protection of love is being built in many ways around the children of northern Uganda. There is an active Church in Uganda, and Christians there have done what they can under the economic and political realities of the country. They are working with Christian relief organizations, but they especially need financial resources. There simply aren't enough people and money to meet the extreme needs.

As Grace Akallo has gone around the United States speaking, and through her appearance on national television and at a congressional committee hearing, people from other countries are beginning to learn about the story of northern Uganda and are joining in a quest to bring healing to this land.

U.S. Representatives Barbara Lee (left, D-CA) and Christopher H. Smith (R-NJ) at a press conference called by Smith to highlight the plight of children in northern Uganda. Smith introduced the Child Soldier Prevention Act of 2006 in the House of Representatives in July 2006. (Photo by Faith McDonnell)

Efforts in North America have included the national tour of *Invisible Children*, a documentary about northern Uganda;

annual walks to raise awareness of and funds for the children of Gulu and elsewhere; and a night when thousands of mostly young people did their own "night commute" in solidarity with the children. Their story has now been told in hearings conducted by the U.S. House of Representatives. Centers have been established to give new hope to as many children as possible and to treat the physical and emotional scars of those who have returned after being abducted.

This chapter will look at a few of the efforts of those advocates who are building a protection of love.

Advocacy and Political Involvement

Uganda Conflict Action Network (Uganda CAN), GuluWalk and World Vision are examples of organizations that work as advocates for peace and justice for the people of northern Uganda. They urge activism by U.S. citizens to push for more political involvement by the U.S. government.

Uganda CAN (ugandacan.org) is an extraordinary venture by young people who are sold out for northern Uganda. It was started in mid-2005 by two University of Notre Dame students, Peter Quaranto and Michael Poffenberger, who had become acquainted with the crisis in northern Uganda when they went to Uganda on a study-abroad program.

The objectives of Uganda CAN are to focus attention of policy makers and the media on the war in northern Uganda, provide up-to-date and accurate news and commentary about northern Uganda and mobilize grassroots support. The goal is a just peace for northern Uganda, which the organization believes can happen with creative strategies and a thoughtful U.S. foreign policy on northern Uganda.

Authors Faith McDonnell (left) and Grace Akallo at the Northern Uganda Lobby Day Symposium at George Washington University, Washington, D.C., October 2006. The lobby day was cosponsored by Uganda CAN, World Vision, Invisible Children, GuluWalk and nine other organizations. (Photo by Crystal Selah)

Uganda CAN works with the Acholi Religious Leaders Peace Initiative and other faith-based indigenous groups in northern Uganda. They always seek to be partners with the Ugandans and to voice their concerns.

An example of the work of Uganda CAN is their efforts in the summer of 2006 to enhance the peace negotiations between the LRA and the government of Uganda with U.S. participation. Uganda CAN worked with Christian leaders in northern Uganda to secure endorsement by U.S. faith-based groups for a letter from the Christian Council in Uganda, asking that the United States send a high-level participant to the peace talks in Juba.

Walking for Peace in Northern Uganda

Working closely with Uganda CAN is GuluWalk (guluwalk. com), an international organization based in Canada. Gulu-

Walk is focused on helping to support the children of northern Uganda with an education and a future. This organization was founded by two young Canadians, Adrian Bradbury and Kieran Hayward, who had first heard of the plight of the children of northern Uganda in the spring of 2005.

Bradbury and Hayward created the GuluWalk as a way to tell the story of northern Uganda's children and to draw attention to their plight. For 31 days in July 2005, they walked 12.5 kilometers into downtown Toronto to sleep in front of city hall. At sunrise, after about four hours of sleep, they returned home. According to the GuluWalk website, they "continued to work full-time and attempted to maintain their usual daily routine, to mimic the lifestyle endured by the Acholi children of northern Uganda."[1] Over the 31 days, Bradbury and Hayward walked 775 kilometers in 154 hours and 18 minutes— 872,739 steps.

GuluWalk has become a worldwide movement. In October 2006, over 30,000 people in 82 cities and 15 different countries participated in GuluWalk 2006. Over $500,000 was raised by GuluWalk 2006 to support the children of northern Uganda.

Uganda CAN cofounder and director Michael Poffenberger prepares to lead the five-mile GuluWalk in Washington, D.C., October 2006.
(Photo by Faith McDonnell)

Counseling Returning Abductees

World Vision International (worldvision.org) is a Christian relief and development organization dedicated to helping children
and their communities worldwide reach their full potential by
tackling the causes of poverty. World Vision has a special bur-
den for the pain that is caused to children in northern Uganda.
Staff of this organization studied the situation and produced a
comprehensive report titled *Pawns of Politics*. Grace Akallo now
works with World Vision.

World Vision launched a campaign to end the child soldier
horrors, issuing the declaration "Children Should Never Be
Soldiers." They are seeking one million signatures for the dec-
laration. They have also created a Children of War Mobilizer's
Toolkit, including a DVD entitled *Caught in the Crossfire:
Uganda's Children of War*.

Their Children of War Rehabilitation Center in Gulu, which
opened in 1995, counsels former child soldiers and works to
bring restoration to their lives. It provides them with temporary shelter, HIV/AIDS education, food, medical treatment,
psychosocial counseling, vocational training and spiritual nur-

Rory Anderson, World Vision's senior policy advisor for Africa,
speaks at the GuluWalk in Washington, D.C., October 2006.
(Photo by Faith McDonnell)

ture and facilitates a smooth reunion of the children with their families.

The builders of the protection of love—those whom God is using to make changes for the children in northern Uganda—are defiant in the face of the deception that says, "There is nothing you can do. People are suffering all over the world. Who do you think you are that that you could make a difference?" They are defiant in the midst of the seductive torpor of resignation that whispers, "This is just the way it is going to be until Jesus returns."

These builders are prophets. They declare the truth that, "No, this is not the Lord's idea of how things should be." They declare that the Kingdom of God is here in us, and that each one of us can make a difference.

They are lovers. They have the eyes of lovers—they see those who are invisible to others. They have the hands of lovers—they work and fight without ceasing for those they love. They speak like lovers—they say, "Arise, my darling, my beautiful one, and come with me. See! The winter is past; the rains are over and gone. Flowers appear on the earth; the season of singing has come, the cooing of doves is heard in our land" (Song of Songs 2:10–12).

They say to the children, "See! We will fight until the winter of Kony is past, until the misery of war is over and gone. We will be beside you until flowers displace land mines in the Acholi earth, until the season of singing takes the place of the mourning and wailing of mothers who have lost their children, and until in the silence of peace you hear the Spirit of God."

Here are more of those who are building love's protection around the children of northern Uganda.

A Village for Children

There is probably no other advocate for northern Uganda quite like Pastor Sam Childers (boyerspond.com), whose kind of faith and determination to serve God will have the last word over Satan concerning the fate of northern Uganda. Pastor Childers is determined that God's people will write a new chapter in the history of northern Uganda. He epitomizes what Bishop Festo Kivengere meant when he said, "Nothing short of the power of [Jesus'] resurrection in the center of our lives makes it possible to meet the onslaughts of the enemy."[2]

Childers is a Christian who is totally committed to the children in northern Uganda and South Sudan. He has provided a home for orphan children and longs to see them all healed from the wounds and trauma of past experiences.

Childers is a former drug dealer and biker gang member turned Christian pastor. At this writing, he has rescued more than five hundred Ugandan and Sudanese children from the LRA. He doesn't wait for the UPDF or the SPLA to bring rescued children to him. He goes out and gets them. He reunites children with parents if the parents are still alive.

Those whose parents have been killed come to live at Childers's orphanage, Children's Village, in Nimule, South Sudan. Children's Village is as secure as is humanly possible. There is a chain-link fence, and armed guards patrol through each night. Childers's own soldiers protect the compound and manage the facility in its day-to-day operations.

The Village is being expanded to give children more room and privacy, something they have never had before. He is now looking for trauma counselors and others who are equipped to help bring healing to the minds and emotions of the children.

Childers had his own construction business (with his drug business on the side) before he turned his life over to Jesus Christ. So he was well-equipped to oversee the building of Children's Village in 2001.

He cleared 36 acres of bush to put up dormitories that now house 110 children. The complex features showers, outhouses and a flush toilet, a small area for pigs and chickens, a cooking area, a church, storage rooms, two security posts and a few guesthouses for visitors. A school building is planned. Care of the children is supervised by women from the village who also cook and clean.

The LRA has threatened that Childers will not die an easy death if they catch him. But Childers has pledged to keep on rescuing children until Kony and the other LRA rebels are brought to justice. He also intends to build an orphanage in the Congo, which also has felt Kony's violence.

The first time Childers came to the region, he saw a boy who had been killed by a land mine. He said of that experience, "As I stood over the child, I cried and wept, and I told the Lord Jesus, I'll do whatever I can do to help these people." He has kept his promise, and American Christians can help him. Donations support the rescue operations and orphanage. People also can pray for his and his associates' protection from the LRA and for the successful rescue of more children.[3]

Invisible Children

One of the most far-reaching and dramatic endeavors on behalf of the night commuter children is the film *Invisible Children* and the organization by the same name that has grown up around it (invisiblechildren.com). *Invisible Children* is making an impact not only politically and socially but also visually and artistically. In addition, the movement has become a kind of cultural phenomenon, a move of the Spirit that embraces everyone who wants to make the world of northern Uganda's children a better place.

Filmmakers Jason Russell, Bobby Bailey and Laren Poole have documented the story of the Acholi children. Their message is that the children of northern Uganda have been invisible to the world at large. The world community has seemed indifferent to whether these children make it through another night without being taken by the LRA.[4]

Russell, Bailey and Poole had been given a rare opportunity for filmmakers: They had been invited to show *Invisible Children* on Capitol Hill. On a cold, early spring day in 2006, they met with interested persons at lunch in the basement of one of the office buildings used by the U.S. Senate. All around them was the daily flow of congressional staff, lobbyists and folks from the senators' home states seeking favors on Capitol Hill.

In the rarefied atmosphere of governmental Washington, the oxygen breathed often seems to be one part diplomacy to two parts appeasement. The wise and learned ones try to slow down the rash and impulsive as naive idealists. There is smiling condescension for those who rage about evil or urge intervention and advocacy to stop injustice. They dismiss advocates as unable to calculate the big-picture consequences of the sort of actions they demand. They have no doubt that their nuanced approach to leadership is far better.

Around one set of tables, Russell and Bailey were sharing their vision with a group of representatives from various Christian and human rights organizations and denominational government relations offices. Some worked for senators and representatives. In some ways it was a historic moment, because it showed that a film about human need could still send out seismic waves through hearts and minds. Those in the Invisible Children organization hope that a couple hundred thousand Americans viewing *Invisible Children* will see for themselves the handiwork of Kony and the LRA rebels. After sharing the tears of one night commuter boy named Jacob, seeing the world of the night commuters and hearing the despair in the voices of displaced Acholi, many will discern that in this crisis there is no room for nuance.

Russell, Bailey and Poole were in Washington to knock on doors of national legislators, in anticipation of a "Global Night Commute" in various cities across the United States on behalf of the northern Ugandan night commuters.

With the filmmakers were a number of young people whose minds were seized by the horrors in northern Uganda. They had volunteered to travel the country on the national tour, showing the movie and acquainting the world with the night commuters. The young adult volunteers have taken the name "roadies" because they live for months at a time in recreation vehicles traveling the roads. The center of interest has been southern California, and one roadie referred to the volunteers as "surfer kids from San Diego." They had put their lives on hold to join the *Invisible Children* road crew, tooling around the United States.

The Invisible Children movement seems to be full of such contradictions and even madness, and not just the madness of three young Americans who rashly hurtled headlong into the cosmos of Joseph Kony with only a camera to defend themselves. It is a buoyant madness, as if it is being propelled by a power beyond human understanding and inviting all who see the film to be mad, too.

Russell was introduced to Africa through a youth mission trip, telling stories in street dramas for kids in slum areas of Kenya. "I talked with Kenyans and sensed each one had stories to tell but no ability to do so. When I graduated from film school, I sensed from God that I should go back."

He talked to his friends Bobby Bailey and Laren Poole until they shared that desire. When they made the first trip to northern Uganda, Russell was 24 years old, and Bailey was 21. Poole turned 20 in Africa.

Russell said it was the children they met who most affected him. It crossed the journalist boundary of objective separation from the story to become friends with the children they were filming. But they also became close to children and got a glimpse of the souls behind the tragedy.

"We couldn't turn our back on our friends," Russell explained. "There was a relationship there. Then you see it's not statistics."

They had planned to interview many night commuters in their documentary. They were setting up and ready to begin work on the first night when a child named Jacob came up to them. He was one of a few who spoke English.

He said, "I have a story. I want to tell you my story." Jacob's story became the central theme of the entire film.

As they filmed an interview with Jacob, Poole remembers, he felt a "huge transition" in his own life. Poole knew that it was not a coincidence that God had sent this boy to help him understand the enormity of the war's impact on lives. That transition came through his friendship with the children who lived with the results of the destruction.

"I remember having feelings that turned from sad to frightened," he mused. "All this war started affecting me. It started to tear me apart, and I felt powerless."

Russell, Bailey and Poole took a year off from work and school for the project. Their progress was slowed because Poole contracted malaria and needed over a month's hospitalization and three months to recuperate. Months were needed to edit the footage. By November 2003 they were ready to make a trailer for prerelease promotion. In June 2004 they rented a movie theater in San Diego for three initial showings. Soon a large California church asked to show it, and its message spread. That November they found themselves in Washington, D.C., invited by the Adoption Institute to show their film at a congressional briefing in the Capitol.

They needed a vehicle accompanying their film that further encouraged public identification with the Acholi, so the newly created Invisible Children organization launched a bracelet campaign. Over the next year they overcame many hurdles to set up a company that employed 125 Acholi people making colorful string bracelets. "The Acholi people are such hard workers," Poole said. "This program gives them dignity."

Invisible Children also began organizing Global Night Commute, which occurred April 29, 2006. Its goal was to help people identify with the lives of the night commuter children. In advance of this event, seven road tour teams spread out across the United States in recreation vehicles. From February 1 until April 29, the teams had a total of more than 700 screenings in 38 states.

All of this culminated in the Night Commute rallies in cities across the United States. Jacob was flown to the United States to the Chicago rally. Ashley Beard was in the Orlando, Florida, Global Night Commute team. She wrote of this "absolutely amazing" experience later:

> It was a hauntingly beautiful sound, signifying the gravity of the situation in Uganda. An emergency is taking place, and I think we conveyed that. With a small inspirational welcome and the police

force ready to roll, the walkers were on their way. . . . Armed with a djembe (African drum) and a new type of confidence, I set out to find anyone willing to listen to its soothing beat. While I was walking around, I was drawn to a group of boys playing guitars and a djembe. . . . I have never played the djembe before, but that night beautiful noises were made. When I sat down, I had no idea of the events that were about to unfold.

All of these endeavors required a more extensive organization, and an important part of the effort has been accomplished by the Invisible Children "roadies" who accompany the film and strengthen its message in tours across North America. Roadies Clint Darrah, Ashley Beard, David Santamaria, Jessica Main, Emily Manassero and Jessica Chan also put their lives on hold.

Instead of working to save money for graduate school, Darrah joined the team for a salary that amounted to fifteen dollars a day, with no medical insurance. He was willing, though, because he had spent some time in Africa, and it has "a way of capturing your heart." Of their work, Darrah writes, "It's not about 'us' going and saving 'them,' but it is very much neighbors extending hands to neighbors, helping to bear one another's burdens."

Darrah said that road teams took the film to show at schools of all descriptions and grade levels, colleges and universities, churches and synagogues, coffee shops, punk rock shows and classical concerts, skate shows, dodgeball tournaments, house parties, Wal-Mart parking lots, parks, bookstores, libraries, Mexican restaurants and even Capitol Hill.

I heard senators say that if we don't act, children will die. I saw the tears of the high schoolers, and I heard the innocent question of ten-year-olds who don't understand how one man can hold 1.8 million Ugandans hostage. Every day, at each of these screenings,

I saw lives changed. I watched the youth of America be inspired as they viewed the film for the first time. I watched their hearts break for Jacob and Tony, and then saw them move into action, by setting up more screenings, helping with the Global Night Commute, holding benefit concerts, and raising thousands of dollars through bake sales (at which I may have eaten too many of their goodies). The efforts were all to end the war in Uganda and put more children through school.

Darrah said he saw the film make an impact on thousands of lives, including his own. People awakened to the realities of their own lives in relation to those of the Acholi. He said people looked upon a grave injustice, and it shook their minds.

Beard participated in the government presentations in Washington, D.C., and found herself frustrated once again by the lack of passion that people who have important responsibilities feel for what they do.

When we were at a briefing, the State Department (representative) was talking about the war in northern Uganda like it was just another day at work. [The official was] spitting out facts about how one thousand people die a week and how this is the worst humanitarian crisis in the world today. . . . I think all these bigwigs forget that these are just not statistics. These are people with hearts, minds, and feelings just like everyone else. . . . How much longer are we going to let this war go on? When will we wake up? How about when the LRA spreads into the Congo and continues its destruction? Maybe the day we wake up and try to end this thing, it will be too late.

Beard said she has been challenging the teens she meets to set aside the magazines and look at things that are important. Young people, she said, need to find a passion and chase after it. "Passions and dreams are what keep us alive, and when you chase after them, a beauty unfolds unlike anything I have ever seen."

Dave Santamaria, another member of the road team, echoed Beard's impatience with people's indifference, saying it distressed him "when we're at a college and tell someone or they walk by an Invisible Children poster and just keep walking or say they have to go do something like watch their favorite TV program."

He believes that the way to get people to care is to convince them that they have a voice to be heard, that they're worth something:

> I got a new perspective [during the Global Night Commute] on what Jesus meant in the Lord's Prayer when He says "on earth as it is in heaven," when everyone is laying down for someone other than themselves. . . . I saw a generation of idealists whose ideas are becoming realities, and we're not even close to being done.

Roadie Jessica Main was considering fashion school, but the children of northern Uganda changed her mind.

Emily Manassero would have been in her second semester at Azusa Pacific University, but she explained her change of plans by saying, "God doesn't call us to live a safe life. [You need] to step outside of the normal American Christian life and pursue what you believe."

In Columbus, Ohio, two Sudanese refugees, now students at Ohio State University, coordinated a Global Night Commute. Simon Dau and Bol Aweng could identify with the lives of northern Uganda's night commuters more than most. They were "Lost Boys," Sudanese children forced to flee to Ethiopia when their villages were attacked by the Sudanese government army. Dau explained that he and Aweng had to fight for justice for the northern Ugandan children because they had experienced what those children had.

Activists Bol B. Aweng, Ben Miller, Melissa Miller and Simon Dau. (Photo by Heather Hart)

On the afternoon of April 29, 2006, participants met at the State House in downtown Columbus and walked to OSU. Dau reported that participants came from all over the Columbus area and included families with small children, as well as students. In all, 788 people became night commuters. They spent the night in a wide-open area known as the Oval and wrote letters to their senators, to the President of the United States and to the UN Security Council, urging them to help restore peace in this region of Uganda that has endured so much suffering.

Jessica Chan, the manager for the *Invisible Children* road tour, has effectively summed up why so many of her peers are filling their hearts with northern Uganda:

> The young people of this country have so much passion and are just waiting for something to come along that will allow them to use it. They've found that materialism is not fulfilling and want something real to hold on to. God has opened their eyes to what's happening in Uganda and is using it to change Americans.

23

Making a Difference

"Welcome to the movement!"

The story of Africa is so fluid that some aspects of the story may be out of date by the time you read this book. At the time of its writing, an extraordinary turn of events is unfolding. The government of the autonomous region of South Sudan was created in the Comprehensive Peace Agreement between the government of Sudan and the Sudan People's Liberation Movement. South Sudan is now sponsoring peace talks between the LRA and the Uganda national government.

No one knows what the outcome will be, but just the fact that they are taking place suggests that some battle is being waged that is beyond that of flesh and blood, beyond the world that we can see with our eyes.

Whatever the current political situation, the wounds in Uganda will take many years to heal. The single most important thing that people can do for the Acholi people and the night commuters is to pray for an end to the twenty-year war; security, peace and restoration for the people; the ability to return and farm their land; rehabilitation and healing of child soldiers; and the rebuilding of broken families.

In Grace's testimony before the House International Relations Committee in April 2006, she spoke about the kinds of things that might make a difference in bringing peace to Uganda. The following are some excerpts from her testimony, following the description of her abduction and escape.

Unfortunately, my story is not uncommon. In fact, it has become so common that abduction is now a fear that daily defines the lives of children who live in the war-affected areas. Because there is no protection for children in northern Uganda, they have created their own way to cope. Thousands of children walk each evening by themselves to towns as far as ten miles away to find safety from the LRA. They sleep on the streets of town centers and in makeshift camps. These children are now known as "night commuters." Recently, there has been a decline in the number of attacks by the LRA, so the number of night commuters has been reduced. But just as the LRA kidnapped me in the middle of the night, they usually abduct children under the cover of darkness. Because of this, most children in northern Uganda are now afraid to sleep in their own beds at night.

This war continues because the world ignores our plight. But this war can stop if leaders in the international community take real action to end this crisis. By action, I specifically mean three things:

1. *High-level engagement by the U.S. government.* Members of Congress, the administration and international leaders must use

their political influence to pressure the government of Sudan to stop supporting the LRA. The U.S. must also use high-level influence to pressure the Ugandan government to end the war.

Remember, more than 80 percent of the LRA is comprised of abducted children—young people like myself who were stolen in the middle of the night.

2. *U.S. leadership in mobilizing the international community, to put global pressure on combatants to protect children and to end the conflict.*

3. *Providing more resources to help people suffering because of this conflict.*

Although the number of rebel attacks has decreased in some areas, many of my family and friends are still living in squalid displacement camps. Those who remain in the IDP camps continue to need significant humanitarian assistance.

In some areas, people have begun to return to their villages, but continued protection and security against the LRA who are still at large is critical. It will also be important for the government of Uganda and the international community to provide returnees with adequate resettlement assistance and support in restoring and developing community infrastructure so that people can begin to rebuild their lives.

We also need support for more psychosocial programs that help all children living in northern Uganda, because all children in the region have been traumatized by this war, whether they have been abducted or watched their brother or sister or classmate being abducted, or they are a "night commuter" and live in fear of abduction.

If these things are done, I believe the war will end. It can end tomorrow if the world comes together to do these things. Mr. Chairman, I ask for your help and the help of others to take action to end this war, so that my sisters and brothers and all the children of northern Uganda can sleep in peace.[1]

Authors Faith McDonnell (right) and Grace Akallo enjoy a moment together prior to Grace's testimony before the House International Relations Committee, April 26, 2006. The committee's hearing was on the topic "The Endangered Children of Northern Uganda." (Photo by Pauline Hildebrandt)

Making a Difference through Prayer

The Uganda People's Defense Force has been mentioned frequently in the course of this book, but you have the opportunity to become part of a stronger, more powerful force: the Northern Uganda Prayer Force. Here are some general prayer topics for northern Uganda:

An end to over two decades of war

Security, peace and restoration for the people

Nearly two million displaced people to be able to return home and to receive back their land

Rehabilitation and healing for child soldiers

Reconciliation for families

Protection, health and wisdom for relief workers and church
leaders

Lives, homes and farms of the people to be rebuilt

You can also pick a topic, such as "the people of northern
Uganda," and pray in more detail. For instance:

Pray for the night commuters, the harassed and abused young
girls, the men and women who have succumbed to despair,
the leaders of the churches in northern Uganda, the relief
workers and volunteers, the children and those who once
were children who have been abducted. Pray that they will
know that God loves them and that Christ died for them.
Pray that they will have the faith of Archbishop Janani
Luwum, of the Ugandan martyrs, of Grace Akallo.

Pray for the persecutors and killers—for the troubled young
boys who have become rapists; for those indifferent or hostile to the Acholi throughout Uganda; and for the rebels of
the LRA, even Kony himself. Pray for the Spirit of God to
convict all of these of their sin and wrongdoing. Pray for
them to acknowledge, confess and repent from their sins.
Pray for them to know they can be forgiven by the God
who loves them even in the midst of their depravity and
violence. Pray for Gulu, Kitgum, Lira, Pader and elsewhere
in northern Uganda to become like the road to Damascus
(see Acts 9): that there will be the striking down of a Joseph
[Kony] and the rising up of a "Paul."

You can also be aware of northern Uganda as you go through
your day. You may wish to pray a short prayer for peace and
justice for the Acholi whenever you think of Uganda, or you

may wish to be in constant prayer. The Russian Orthodox Christians are famous for the Jesus Prayer: *Lord Jesus Christ, Son of God* (prayed while breathing in), *have mercy on me, a sinner* (prayed while breathing out). Praying in this manner allows you to obey the biblical command to "pray without ceasing" (1 Thessalonians 5:17, NKJV). You can create your own Jesus Prayer for northern Uganda: *Lord Jesus Christ, Son of God, have mercy on the children of northern Uganda*, or pray whatever is on your heart. Soon your prayers will become as natural as breathing.

Find northern Uganda on a globe or in an atlas and pray for the land as you study its topography. Research northern Uganda on the Internet (a list of websites is included in this chapter) and watch for it on television news and in the newspaper. Use the information you read and hear to inform your prayers.

Search the Bible for Scripture passages about justice, peace, oppression and the promises of God. Pray those Scriptures for Uganda and all of Africa.

If you like music from around the world, you may wish to find some Ugandan or other African music and worship songs. Think and pray about northern Uganda as you hear and sing the songs. If you go to a liturgical church, ask your pastor if you can use liturgy from a Ugandan church for one of your services.

Start a Northern Uganda Prayer Force at your church, in your college dorm or after school, with your women's group, with your men's group, with a group that prays for children or with friends. Meet and pray on a regular basis for northern Uganda, using specific prayer points gathered through ongoing research, and keep up with the news.

Making a Difference through Political Advocacy

Grace stresses the importance of involving the international community in the war. The Uganda and Sudan governments are sensitive to world opinion, and they can be motivated to end their fighting and/or stop supporting the insurgencies. In the United States, this can best be accomplished through personal petition of government officials, including the president, senators and congressional representatives. The office of the President of the United States is: The White House, 1600 Pennsylvania Avenue NW, Washington, D.C. 20500. Telephone comments to the President can be directed to 202-456-1111 or to the switchboard at 202-456-1414. The number to send fax messages to the President is 202-456-2461.

To find addresses for U.S. national legislators, go to the websites house.gov and senate.gov. Phone their offices to voice immediate concerns. In the United States, telephone numbers are available through the national government switchboard at 202-224-2131. Inform them of your concern for what is happening in northern Uganda.

If there is any legislation on northern Uganda, ask your representative and senators if they are cosponsors, and if not, why not. If and when there is legislation being offered on northern Uganda, contact other senators and representatives outside your district and state. Such a bill would likely go through the House International Relations Committee or the Senate Foreign Relations Committee.

Write to the U.S. Department of State, to the secretary of state, to the assistant secretary for African Affairs or to the ambassador at the Office to Monitor Trafficking in Persons. Names and addresses are at the website state.gov.

Sometimes the best way to be heard by persons in the executive and legislative levels of U.S. government is through a Washington-based human rights or other advocacy group that is concerned with northern Uganda. They will tell you when there is a particularly urgent matter about which to contact the President, and you can participate in their work. Most of these groups have access to the White House Office of Public Liaison. You will find contact information for some of these groups in this chapter.

Write to the Ugandan ambassador to your country or the ambassadors to the United Nations and Uganda. The Ugandan embassy in Washington, D.C., has a website, ugandaembassy. com, and the U.S. embassy in Kampala is at kampala.usembassy. gov/. These sites will list the names of current ambassadors.

Through such avenues, you can be a voice for the night commuters, the child soldiers and the displaced persons, one who is heard at the highest levels of Uganda's government. Write to the media. You can write a letter to the editor of your local newspaper, and it is increasingly effective to write email to influential blogs. Make the invisible children visible to your community.

In an era of increasing celebrity activism for international causes, consider writing to your favorite music group, Christian or secular. Because he found out about the persecution of Christians in South Sudan years ago, Christian singer and songwriter Michael Card invited a southern Sudanese refugee to go with him on tour and speak about Sudan at every concert for a number of years.

Suggest specific ideas or draft bills for resolutions at national denominational conventions or assemblies. If your church is not affiliated with a denomination, the resolution could even come from your local church and be sent to the media and government.

Many sources of information and avenues of involvement are available if you know where to look. For example, on the Invisible Children website you can subscribe to the email list, staying informed about the next Global Night Commute and national tour. The following is a directory of activist websites (Christian and secular) through which you can become better informed about northern Uganda and participate in the work of God in Africa.

amnesty.org

boyerspond.com

crisisgroup.org

farreachingministries.org

guluwalk.com

hrw.org

irinnews.org

invisiblechildren.com

ird-renew.org

namecampaign.org

ugandacan.org

ugandamission.org

worldvision.org

Create a bulletin board in your church, Sunday school room, dorm, campus lounge, youth group area or blog, or wherever else you can, to post information and current news about northern Uganda.

Write to family and friends about the plight of the children in northern Uganda. You could send cards or create an email distribution list. Ask family and friends to pray and to write letters of their own to officials. Ask them if they would consider their own email distribution list for passing on the word about northern Uganda.

If you haven't done it already, it's time to see a movie. *Invisible Children: Rough Cut* is available from invisiblechildren.com. Another story about the plight of the Acholi is the Canadian film *Uganda Rising*. This new film has already won numerous awards at international film festivals. It is available for purchase at ugandarising.com. Arrange for a screening at your church, your synagogue, your school, your community center, your extended family reunion—wherever there is a large gathering of people to whom you can spread the message.

In addition to participating in such public events as the Global Night Commute or GuluWalk, you may wish to participate in a national event such as a prayer rally, a candlelight vigil, a demonstration or a protest. Keep in touch with advocacy organizations for the national events.

Locally, you could have a prayer vigil on the anniversary of the death of the Uganda martyrs or of Archbishop Janani Luwum. Another idea would be to have a commemoration service for a particular IDP camp or other location on the anniversary of

People of any age can participate in a rally, walk or demonstration for northern Uganda. At the GuluWalk, participants came as young as eleven-year-old Fiona McDonnell, here awaiting the commencement of the walk with friend Carolynne Rine. (Photo by Faith McDonnell)

one of the massacres by the LRA. The purpose is to commemorate but also to focus attention on northern Uganda. You can show the public the connection between the death of the young Ugandan martyrs at the hand of King Mwanga and the LRA's tragic abduction and killing of young northern Ugandans today. The killing of Archbishop Luwum and thousands of others by Idi Amin can be compared to the killings by Joseph Kony. Find a connection and make the most of it.

Providing for Needs

Not all of the problems of northern Uganda are political. Deep wounds exist in people that can never be resolved by government or fixed with large financial expenditures. The wounds of recent history are in the fabric of life that has passed to the next generation. But God is bringing healing. Unlike Alice Auma's false "Lakwena" healing spirit, the Holy Spirit is the Spirit of truth, and He is at work in northern Uganda. In the midst of wrenching poverty, the Church in northern Uganda is living on faith in Jesus Christ, attempting to bring comfort and assurance of God's love to the people.

As described above, Acholi religious leaders, including Christian pastors, have become effective advocates to promote peace. They are the foremost Ugandan advocates for the displaced persons and child soldiers. Because the churches exist with almost no financial resources, Western Christians can be enormously effective by giving financially to a denomination's churches there or the northern Uganda Christian Church as a whole.

Money to Ugandan churches supports a mainstay of civil society for the Acholi. A little money goes an extraordinarily long way in Uganda. There are many fund-raising projects that provide very concrete needs. For information on these projects, contact Uganda CAN, World Vision or other assistance groups, such as Lutheran World Services or Catholic Relief Services.

The Anglican Church of Uganda sponsors several programs that help educate children and provide for teachers and native ministry workers. Even bicycles and motorcycles to get pastors around the country are needed.

Other needs include school uniforms, books and desks; salaries for teachers and school funds for pastors' children; sewing machines for a tailoring teaching lab; and sewing supplies for an income-generating project for pastors' wives.

You may also wish to become an intercessor for the ministry of American missionaries in Uganda such as Phil and Jennifer Leber (ugandamission.org). The Lebers have a ministry of teaching and discipleship to young men and women who are the future leaders of Uganda. They work directly for the archbishop of the Church of Uganda, a nine-million-member province of the worldwide Anglican Communion, throughout the country's 31 dioceses. Jennifer Leber is working to bring relief to the night commuters by raising public awareness of the plight of the thousands of desperate children in Kitgum. Her projects include a tailoring school, a counseling center and night commuter shelters in Kitgum.

It is possible through aid organizations to personally go to northern Uganda as a Bible teacher, English teacher, health worker, art therapist, trauma counselor or construction overseer. People are needed to serve in many capacities, and there are opportunities for short-term mission workers. One identified need is for Christians to host conferences for the pastors who live at the IDP camps.

It's our job to find out where and how God is calling us to be part of the movement that is making history for northern

Uganda. It's up to us to find the place where our gifts and passions can be used.

Not many are called to join Sam Childers in the rescue of northern Ugandan children abducted by the LRA, but people are frequently called to join a Global Night Commute. Not many will see the wards full of night commuters at St. Joseph's Mission Hospital in Kitgum, but many can care that they are there.

But I am so weak! I don't have much faith. I like being comfortable. Is that what you are thinking? Remember the comforting news Paul gives us in 1 Corinthians 1:20–31 — God will use the weak things of this world to shame the strong.

So if you're weak, welcome to the movement! This movement for northern Uganda is comprised of the mad and the weak, the passionate and the prayerful, the prophets and the lovers. Such lives can rewrite the history of northern Uganda.

Authors Faith McDonnell (right) and Grace Akallo in the shadow of the U.S. Capitol during Grace's trip to Washington, D.C., to testify before Congress. (Photo by Pauline Hildebrandt)

Notes

Chapter 2: Stolen in the Darkness

1. The LRA has also attacked in southern Sudan, assisting the Sudanese government in destabilizing and terrorizing the people. In most recent years, they have also entered the Democratic Republic of Congo (DRC) and attacked civilians there.

2. J. Carter Johnson, "Deliver Us from Kony: Why the Children of Uganda Are Killing One Another in the Name of the Lord," *Christianity Today*, January 2006, 31.

3. The Republic of Uganda Ministry of Health, "Health and Mortality Survey among Internally Displaced Persons in Gulu, Kitgum, and Pader Districts, Northern Uganda," theirc.org/resources/N-20Uganda-20MOH-20Survey-20 Report-20July-202005-20FINAL.

4. World Vision, *Pawns of Politics: Children, Conflict, and Peace in Northern Uganda*, 2nd ed. (World Vision International, 2005), 4.

5. Ibid., 18.

Chapter 4: Fire of Martyrdom

1. F. A. Forbes, *Planting the Faith in Darkest Africa: The Life Story of Father Simeon Lourdel*, History 29, ch. 8, the pelicans.co.uk/.

2. *The Holy Martyrs of Uganda*, magnificat.ca/cal/engl/06-03 (accessed August 4, 2006).

3. Forbes, *Planting the Faith*, ch. 6.

4. Converts who are being instructed in the tenets of the Christian faith to prepare for baptism.

5. Forbes, *Planting the Faith*, ch. 7.

6. Ibid.

7. Ibid.

8. Mission Office, Diocese of Los Angeles, missionsla.org/subpages/learn/archivesaint/marchsaint (accessed August 3, 2006).

9. *Holy Martyrs of Uganda*.

10. Ibid.

11. Forbes, *Planting the Faith*, ch. 8.

12. Ibid.

13. Timothy C. Morgan, "Africa's Azusa Street," ChristianityToday.com (27 March 2006).

14. Julie Katarobo, "Blowing on the Ashes of Revival," *Church Mission Society*, 2 September 2005.

15. Charles V. Taylor, "Balance," pastornet.net.au/renewal/journal7/taylor (accessed August 3, 2006).

Chapter 6: A New Darkness Descends

1. Bruce Harris, "Heroes and Killers of the Twentieth Century: Idi Amin," moreorless.au.com/killers/amin.#kills (accessed August 4, 2006).
2. Ibid.
3. "Idi Amin," Wikipedia online encyclopedia, en.wikipedia.org/wiki/Idi_Amin_Dada (accessed November 8, 2006).
4. Harris, "Heroes and Killers."
5. Ibid.
6. "Idi Amin."
7. Ibid.
8. "The Excessive Kindness of Islam," Satyameva Jayate website, flex.com/~jai/satyamevajayate/loot (accessed November 8, 2006).
9. Manfred R. Lehmann, "Entebbe Rescue Operation 20th Anniversary," manfredlehmann.com/sieg184 (accessed November 8, 2006).
10. Ibid.
11. "IDF's Daring Rescue of Jewish Hostages Held at Entebbe, Uganda," The Wednesday Report 18.26 (23 June 2004), thewednesdayreport.com/twr/twr26v18 (accessed November 8, 2006).
12. "Excessive Kindness."
13. James E. Kiefer, "Janani Luwum, Archbishop of Uganda, Martyr," *Biographical Sketches of Memorable Christians of the Past,* justus.anglican.org/resources/bio/101 (accessed November 8, 2006).
14. Georg Piwang, "Shining the Light of Janani Luwum," Archbishop Janani Luwum Trust, jananiluwumtrust.com/luwum (accessed November 8, 2006).
15. "In an Age of Dictators," westminster-abbey.org (August 4, 2006).
16. Piwang, "Shining the Light."
17. Ibid.
18. "In an Age of Dictators: Janani Luwum," Westminster Abbey tour notes, "Twentieth Century Martyrs." westminster-abbey.org/tour/martyrs/3_jt (accessed August 4, 2006). Archbishop Luwum is one of ten twentieth-century martyrs memorialized in statues on the west-front facade of Westminster Abbey in London.
19. Kiefer, "Janani Luwum."
20. "In an Age of Dictators."
21. Kiefer, "Janani Luwum."
22. "Janani Luwum," Wikipedia online encyclopedia, en.wikipedia.org/wiki/Janani_Luwum (accessed November 8, 2006).
23. Peter Stanway, "Revival in Africa," the Way Christian Ministries website, thewaycm/content/templates/spiritual.aspx?a=110&z=14&page=6 (accessed August 4, 2006).

Chapter 8: Killing as the Spirit Leads

1. Macleod Baker Ochola II, "The Roots of Conflict with a Special Reference to Africa" (manuscript of lecture, National Conference of the Medical Association for the Prevention of War, Victoria, Australia, March 16, 2003), mapw.org.au/conferences/mapw2003/papers/03-16ochola (accessed November 11, 2006).
2. Ibid.
3. Ibid.
4. Ibid.
5. "Northern Uganda: Understanding and Solving the Conflict," International Crisis Group Africa Report #77, April 14, 2004.
6. Ochola, "Roots of Conflict."
7. Heike Behrend, *Alice Lakwena and the Holy Spirits* (Oxford: James Currey Ltd., 1999), 23.
8. "Northern Uganda."
9. Ibid.

10. Ibid.
11. Ibid.
12. Behrend, *Alice Lakwena and the Holy Spirits*, 24.
13. "Northern Uganda."
14. Ibid.
15. Ibid.
16. Behrend, *Alice Lakwena and the Holy Spirits*, 131.
17. Ochola, "Roots of Conflict."
18. Behrend, *Alice Lakwena and the Holy Spirits*, 106.
19. Ibid., 131.
20. Ibid.
21. Ibid., 132.
22. Rosalind I. J. Hackett, "Who Goes to Gulu? The Lord's Resistance Army and the Forgotten War in Uganda," *Peace Colloquy* 6 (Summer 2004), 13.
23. Behrend, *Alice Lakwena and the Holy Spirits*, 132.
24. Ibid., 30.
25. Ibid., 32.
26. Ibid., 33.
27. Ibid., 30.
28. Ibid.
29. Ibid., 31.
30. Ibid., 132.
31. Ibid., 25–26.
32. Ibid., 132.
33. Ibid., 26.
34. Ibid., 57.
35. Ibid., 50.
36. Ibid., 136.
37. Ibid., 59.
38. Ibid., 79–80.
39. Steve Rabey, "'Terrorizing the Innocents in Uganda: Religion Plays a Role in Deadly Lord's Resistance Army," *Christian Research Journal* 28, no. 2 (2005), equip.org/free/JAL110 (accessed November 11, 2006).
40. Behrend, *Alice Lakwena and the Holy Spirits*, 81.
41. Ibid., 58.
42. Ibid., 56–57.
43. Ibid., 93.

Chapter 10: Lakwena Seeks a New Home

1. Behrend, *Alice Lakwena and the Holy Spirits*, 175.
2. Anna Borzello, "Profile: Ugandan Rebel Joseph Kony," BBC News, 5 July 2006.
3. Ibid.
4. Hackett, "Who Goes to Gulu?" 14.
5. Borzello, "Profile: Ugandan Rebel Joseph Kony."
6. Behrend, *Alice Lakwena and the Holy Spirits*, 85.
7. Ibid., 86.
8. Ibid.
9. Ibid., 178.
10. Ibid.
11. Ibid.
12. Ibid., 179.
13. Ibid.
14. Ibid.
15. Ibid., 180.
16. Ibid., 181.
17. Ibid., 186.
18. Ibid., 187.
19. Ibid.
20. Rabey, "Terrorizing the Innocents."
21. Behrend, *Alice Lakwena and the Holy Spirits*, 188.
22. Ibid., 189.
23. Ibid.
24. Herb McMullan, "Living on Faith in East Africa," The Institute on Religion and Democracy, ird-renew .org/site/apps/s/content.asp?c=fvKVLfM VIsG&b=494491&ct=416911.
25. Ochola, "Roots of Conflict."
26. Amnesty International, "Breaking God's Commands: The Destruction of Childhood by the Lord's Resistance Army," Amnesty International Report, September 18, 1997, web.amnesty.org/ library/Index/ENGAFR590011997?ope n&of=ENG-SDN (accessed November 11, 2006).

27. Ibid.
28. Ibid.
29. Ibid.
30. Ibid.
31. Ochola, "Roots of Conflict." Winifred Ochola's death came ten years after the death of their nineteen-year-old daughter, Joyce. Joyce committed suicide after being raped by LRA troops.

Chapter 12: Creating Killer Children

1. Johnson, "Deliver Us from Kony."
2. "Northern Uganda."
3. Johnson, "Deliver Us from Kony."
4. Human Rights Watch, "Human Rights Abuses by the Lord's Resistance Army," in "Uganda: Abducted and Abused," *Human Rights Watch Reports* 15, no. 12 (July 2003). hrw.org/reports/2003/uganda0703/uganda0703a-04.htm#P318_55923 (accessed November 1, 2006).
5. Integrated Regional Information Networks (IRIN), "When the Sun Sets We Start to Worry," IRINnews.org, irin news.org/webspecials/northernuganda/overview (accessed November 1, 2006).
6. Rabey, "Terrorizing the Innocents."
7. Human Rights Watch, "The Scars of Death: Children Abducted by the Lord's Resistance Army in Uganda," Human Rights Watch Children's Rights Project, September 1997.
8. Johnson, "Deliver Us from Kony."
9. Ibid.
10. Joyce Neu, "Conflict Analysis for the Northern Uganda Peace Initiative," Report of the President's Peace Team, March 16, 2006, 6–7.
11. "Northern Uganda."
12. J. Carter Johnson, "Brutality Therapy," *Christianity Today*, January 1, 2006, ctlibrary.com/ct/2006/January/18.30 (accessed November 16, 2006).

13. Johnson, "Deliver Us from Kony."
14. World Vision International, "World Vision's Work in Uganda," World Vision, worldvision.org/worldvision/wvu susfo.nsf/stable/globalissues_uganda_wv work (accessed November 11, 2006).
15. World Vision, *Pawns of Politics*.
16. See theirc.org/.
17. Johnson, "Deliver Us from Kony."
18. Ibid.
19. Ibid.

Chapter 14: Experiences That Leave Scars

1. Human Rights Watch, "Scars of Death."
2. Tim Judah, "Uganda: The Secret War," *New York Review of Books* 51, no. 14 (23 September 2004): 2.
3. Judah, "Uganda: The Secret War," 2.
4. United States Department of State, "Country Narratives: Uganda," Trafficking in Persons Report, June 2006, state.gov/g/tip/rls/tiprpt/2006/65990 (accessed November 1, 2006).
5. Behrend, *Alice Lakwena and the Holy Spirits*, 194.
6. Amnesty International, "Breaking God's Commands."
7. Johnson, "Deliver Us from Kony."
8. Human Rights Watch, "Scars of Death."
9. Amnesty International, "Breaking God's Commands."

Chapter 16: Who Is Protecting Us?

1. Olara A. Otunnu, "Death of a People," *Christian Century* (18 April 2006): 11.
2. Ibid., 11.
3. The Baroness Lady Caroline Cox, deputy speaker of the House of Lords

and founder of the Christian advocacy organization Christian Solidarity World-wide (CSW), recently formed a Christian relief and development organization called HART (Humanitarian Aid Relief Trust). Baroness Cox and a team from HART visited northern Uganda in February 2006.

4. Caroline Cox, HART Visit to Uganda and Sudan, February 6–13, 2006, Preliminary Draft Report.

5. Otunnu, "Death of a People," 11.

6. World Health Organization, "Health and Mortality Survey among Internally Displaced Persons in Gulu, Kitgum, and Pader Districts, Northern Uganda," who.int/hac/crises/uga/sitreps/Ugandamortsurvey.

7. Michelle Brown, Testimony to the House International Relations Committee, "Northern Uganda: Urgent Measures Needed to Address the LRA Threat to Regional Peace and Security," April 26, 2006.

8. Cox, HART Visit to Uganda and Sudan.

9. World Vision, *Pawns of Politics*.

10. Integrated Regional Information Networks (IRIN), "Life at Point Zero," IRINnews.org, irinnews.org/webspecials/northernuganda/sec2 (July 26, 2006).

11. World Vision, *Pawns of Politics*.

12. Ibid.

13. Ibid.

14. IRIN, "Life at Point Zero."

15. Ibid.

16. World Vision, *Pawns of Politics*.

17. Judah, "Uganda: The Secret War," 3.

18. "Counting the Cost: Twenty Years of War in Northern Uganda," Civil Society Organisations for Peace in Northern Uganda (30 March 2006).

19. "Vincent Otti Gave Order for Atiak Massacre," New Vision Uganda Government website, April 20, 2006,

newvision.co.ug/D/8/540/494338 (accessed November 1, 2006).

20. The Atiak trading center was a precursor to the IDP camps. People from the rural areas had moved into trading centers for protection against rebel attacks. Later they were moved to camps.

21. "Focus on LRA Attack on Barlonyo IDPs Camp," IRINnews.org, November 16, 2006, irinnews.org/print.asp?ReportID=39678 (accessed November 16, 2006).

22. Amnesty International, "Government Should Address Attacks on Citizens Urgently," ReliefWeb, February 24, 2004, reliefweb.int/rw/rwb.nsf/AllDocsByUNID/57566716a53aa20185256e4400732c32 (accessed November 1, 2006).

23. Integrated Regional Information Networks (IRIN), "Humanitarian Crisis Persists in Northern Region," ReliefWeb, November 17, 2004, reliefweb.int/rw/rwb.nsf/AllDocsByUNID/0cbcc6cab3a2f1ae85256f4f005f64fc (accessed November 16, 2006).

24. Ibid.

25. Ibid.

26. World Vision UK, "City of Fear," November 16, 2006, worldvision.org.uk/server.php?show=nav.465 (accessed November 16, 2006).

27. Carlos Rodriguez, "Everything Acholi Is Dying," Friends for Peace in Africa, friendsforpeaceinafrica.org/index.php?option=com_content&task=view&id=46&Itemid=77 (accessed November 1, 2006).

28. Olara A. Otunnu, "Nation in Crisis Thanks to Divisive Regime," All Africa.com, September 19, 2006, allafrica.com/stories/200609190945 (accessed November 1, 2006).

29. Grace Akallo, "The Endangered Children of Northern Uganda," testimony before the U.S. House of Representatives International Relations Com-

mittee, Subcommittee on Africa, Global Human Rights and International Operations, April 26, 2006, internationalrelations.house.gov/archives/109/ake042606 (accessed November 1, 2006).

Chapter 18: Acts of Defiance

1. The stories of Prossy and Lilian are from Integrated Regional Information Networks (IRIN), "Waiting for the Light," IRINnews.org. irinnews.org/web specials/northernuganda/overview (accessed November 1, 2006).
2. Tear Fund, "Flood of Night Commuter Children Rises in Northern Uganda," June 2004, tearfund.org/News/Press+release+archive/June+2004/Flood+of+night+commuter+children+rises+in+Northern+Uganda (accessed November 17, 2006).
3. Women's Commission for Refugee Women and Children, "Resilience in the Darkness: An Update on Child and Adolescent Night Commuters in Northern Uganda," February 2005.
4. Ibid.
5. Women's Commission for Refugee Women and Children, "No Safe Place to Call Home: Child and Adolescent Night Commuters in Northern Uganda," July 2004, 3.
6. Ibid., 5.
7. Women's Commission, "Resilience in the Darkness," 6.
8. Ibid., 13.
9. IRIN, "Waiting for the Light."
10. Wes Bentley, quoted in J. Carter Johnson, "Deliver Us from Kony."
11. Keith Morrison, "Coming Back from Uganda a Changed Man," MSNBC blog, August 21, 2005, msnbc.msn.com/id/8974860/#050821a (accessed November 1, 2006).
12. Ibid.
13. Carolyn Davis, "A Ugandan Child Helps Restore Faith," *The Phila-*delphia Inquirer webpage Philly.com, May 10, 2005, philly.com/mld/inquirer/news/editorial/12593929 (accessed November 16, 2006).
14. Ibid.
15. Ibid.

Chapter 20: The Adults Are Not Around

1. Women's Commission, "Resilience in the Darkness."
2. Ibid.
3. IRIN, "Waiting for the Light."
4. Ibid.
5. Women's Commission, "Resilience in the Darkness," 8.
6. Women's Commission, "No Safe Place to Call Home," 9.
7. IRIN, "Waiting for the Light."
8. Women's Commission, "Resilience in the Darkness," 8.
9. Ibid.
10. Women's Commission, "No Safe Place," 10.
11. Ibid., 11.
12. Ibid.
13. Ibid., 12.

Chapter 21: Finding Life Again

1. Els De Temmerman, *Aboke Girls: Children Abducted in Northern Uganda* (Kampala, Uganda: Fountain, 2001).
2. Henk Rossouw, "An African Tale: First Hell, Then College," *The Chronicle of Higher Education*, August 8, 2003, A32–35.
3. Akallo, "The Endangered Children of Northern Uganda." A portion of this testimony is reproduced in chapter 23.

Chapter 22: Hearts Full of Northern Uganda

1. Adrian Bradbury, "2005 Gulu-Walk," http://guluwalk.com/history, (December 3, 2006).

2. Lausanne World Pulse.com, December 2005, lausanneworldpulse .com/12-2005 (accessed November 16, 2006).

3. For more on Sam Childers and Children's Village, see Maria Silwa, "Former Drug Dealer Frees Children in Sudan and Uganda," Christianity.com, christianity.com/religiontoday/1356804.

4. The Invisible Children website is invisiblechildren.com. Quotations and information in this section are based on interviews conducted by Faith McDonnell with film producers and others in the organization.

Chapter 23: Making a Difference

1. Akallo, "The Endangered Children of Northern Uganda."

Index

234

As Religious Liberty Programs Director at the Institute on Religion and Democracy (ird-renew.org), **Faith J. H. McDonnell** works to inform U.S. Christians about the persecution of believers around the world. Now an Anglican, she was raised in the Salvation Army.

Faith speaks widely on the subject of persecuted Christians to church and civic groups and in radio and television interviews. She co-organized rallies in support of Sudan's persecuted Christians in front of the White House, the Canadian Embassy and the Sudanese Embassy, and she coordinated a seven-day prayer vigil for Sudan outside the U.S. State Department. She has drafted legislation on religious persecution for the Episcopal Church and the U.S. Congress and has written for a number of national publications.

Faith's work on Sudan policy brought her knowledge of the atrocities being committed by Joseph Kony and the Lord's Resistance Army in northern Uganda. This then became another area of advocacy for the Institute on Religion and Democracy.

Listening to the music of Irish rockers is what gets Faith and her husband, Francis, moving on those rare free Saturday mornings. With daughter Fiona, Faith shares a love for dogs, cats and *Nancy Drew*. She, Francis and Fiona all love to romp with their black Labrador retriever, Moses.

Grace Akallo was raised with three sisters and one brother in Kaberikale, a small village in Kaberamaido District in Uganda. After helping her mother in the field, she would walk ten miles to and from elementary school. She later went to St. Mary's College, a high school for girls, in Aboke, another small village in Lira District.

In 1996 Grace was dragged away from school to Sudan by the brutal rebel group that had been fighting against the government and people of Uganda since 1986. After much suffering and torture, she escaped and went back to St. Mary's College.

In 2002 she attended Uganda Christian University and two years later transferred to Gordon College in Massachusetts. She also completed an internship at World Vision. As of this writing, she will graduate in May 2007 with a degree in communications, and she hopes to go to graduate school to pursue a degree in international relations and conflict relations.

In 2004 Grace spoke in front of the Amnesty International Annual Meeting and appeared on *Oprah*. In April 2006, she testified in front of Congress. She has spoken in different schools and in a symposium organized by nongovernmental organizations such as World Vision to advocate for the people of northern Uganda.